The Strategy

Debbie Martin

Pen Press

© Debbie Martin 2013

All rights reserved

No part of this publication may be reproduced, stored in a retrieval system, or transmitted in any form or by any means, without the prior permission in writing of the publisher, nor be otherwise circulated in any form of binding or cover other than that in which it is published and without a similar condition including this condition being imposed on the subsequent purchaser.

First published in Great Britain

All paper used in the printing of this book has been made from wood grown in managed, sustainable forests.

ISBN13: 978-1-78003-583-3

Pen Press is an imprint of
Indepenpress Publishing Limited
25 Eastern Place
Brighton
BN2 1GJ

A catalogue record of this book is available from the British Library

Cover design by Staunch Design

Chapter 1: The strategy - whats, whys, wheres and hows...

'Of course, I'm a bit of a loose cannon, you know.' He smirked at me with that sideways look he had that implied 'loose cannon' actually meant 'chase me, chase me...' I thought, 'I am chasing you, you're just not noticing!'

He continued his tale, telling me about the hot blonde who he'd been flirting with the other day. He was obviously desperate for more, but she'd played hard to get and had plainly immensely enjoyed immensely leaving him just hanging - although not without accepting his number before she wiggled seductively away. No man ever seemed to do that with me. I was no different to the hot woman who'd walked casually away from him the other day, but without ever being perceived as 'hot' in Pete's eyes, judging from the amount of attention he gave me. I looked at his face, square-jawed and handsome, sparkling brown eyes, wicked smile, blonde hair curling close to his head in a way that made you want to run your fingers through it. 'Charisma,' I thought – that's what he has, and I don't. And then it all fell into place. I needed a plan – a strategy: **how to get the guy...**

Guys and gals, dicks and chicks - men and women, that is - how different are we? Are we that different at all? The men tell horror stories about dreadful dates with dames and the women about monstrous meets with men, but what defines what we are all looking for? Love, I supposed; but was love - falling in love - the same for men and women? Did it happen the same way? Were there different things that made it happen for each sex? Listening to Pete, I knew the odds on him being interested in me were currently about zero to 1. Why? I was only mid-thirties, intelligent, attractive and quite successful in my career, but... still single. And worse than that, here I was chatting, smiling, flirting for all I was worth with this guy I REALLY fancied and nothing was happening. In fact he was telling me about some girl HE fancied – how bad was that! Could I work out a strategy that would enable me to beat the odds and create the perfect solution: a sure fire way of him begging to be in a relationship with me?

    I applied some reasoning to it. Life is made up of assumptions and expectations; for instance we assume we know the way somewhere because we've been there once before. The expectation is that we'll arrive at the same place in good time without having to check the map, because we assume we remember the way. Do we? Did we? Maybe we do sometimes - with a bit of luck, and a fair wind behind us. More often though, our assumptions take us down a side road and we struggle to find the correct way to get back on track when we finally realise we got lost. This is probably why, I, and many other geographically-challenged women (and men) like me, use a Satnav - but that is by the by. It's a very easy analogy to translate into the road of life, and the relationship route on it.

I decided first it was time to revisit me, and what I was all about - and WHY this just wasn't working!

First of all: the whys? Well I suppose there were a number of 'whys':

- Why did I want a guy?
- Why did I want THIS particular guy?
- Why wasn't he interested in me? He liked me in a roundabout way but, here I was in friend zone…
- Why did I get relegated to friend's zone in the first place?
- Why if he didn't like me in the right way, did I never meet anyone who did?

Then there were some 'whats':

- What was the matter with me?…Ouch, that one felt quite uncomfortable!
- What was I doing wrong?
- What should I be doing instead?
- What exactly was I aiming to achieve?

Then there were the 'how's':

- How do I change my behaviour pattern, if that is the problem?
- How do I change men's perception of me?
- How do I find the kind of man I would like to meet?

- How do I convince him he's interested in ME?
- (of course this included Pete at the time) How did I get Pete to be interested in me?)
- How did I keep them interested?

And finally there were the 'wheres':

- Where do I go to do any of this…?
- Where will I find the information to complete my strategy?

Pete was still talking about the blonde by the time I'd summarised my strategy needs in my head so I tuned in to see what was making him linger on her for so long,

'…but she said she was busy then so I've got to call her again next week…'

It was clear he **was** going to call her next week, even though he'd been unflatteringly told to wait. Why was that, I wondered. Well I don't know - ask him instead, you idiot, I told myself.

'…and will you?'

'Oh of course…'

'Why of course?'

'Well she has style, high value.'

High value? I made a mental note. Let's start with that then…

Chapter 2: High value - the guy blueprint

I have to admit I didn't listen too well to what Pete was saying for most of the rest of that evening, but what did it matter by then? I was so firmly in the dreaded **_friend zone_** that I could have talked about football or the merits of fishnets versus seamed stockings and he wouldn't have been interested. He rambled on more about the amazing blonde and then the wonderful brunette from the week before and I rambled though my thoughts, picking out the ones that seemed to stand out dramatically and say 'pick me, pick me!' like the way we desperately waited for someone to pick us for the netball team at school. However the 'high value' beat all the rest hands down as a starting point, so I decided to get as much information from Pete as I could - after all he was plainly quite content to tell me all about his dates in fine detail, why not use the information for my plan? With knowledge comes power...

It started with Pete's stories about the series of naïve, needy and negative ladies he'd dated. I looked across at the big screen on the pub wall as it was showing a clip from a rom-com currently showing on the TV - about a girl who always made a mess of her dates. Was that me... no, get back onto the subject!

'So Pete, what is the worst date you've ever been on?'

'Oh, don't get me started on that...' But he barely stopped to draw breath before continuing, keen to get started after all.

'One of my first internet dates of all - the woman from Saffron Waldron...' He made it sound as if I should know her from the dramatic intent his tone conveyed, but of course I didn't , unless he'd already told me about her whilst my attention was wandering. I simply smiled encouragingly and he obligingly carried on with enthusiasm. It must be like one of those fishing stories some guys like to tell.

'... it all started with a bit of dialogue on the dating site and we ended up agreeing to meet for a drink the following Saturday. Then she asked me if I could pick her up from her house. Well, I mean - I didn't know her and she didn't know me and I thought *you're not supposed to do that*, but I picked her up anyway and we had a good evening. Then at the end of it, she asked if I wanted to go back for a coffee. I thought again *you're not supposed to do that* but I went back anyway. She went off to make the coffee and then came back wearing just a negligee thing. I drank my coffee and just went - Christ!'

I couldn't help laughing at his comic expression but it did take me back to that throw-away comment earlier - 'high value'. Well she clearly hadn't been, so I started off rule number one in the strategy:

Values :

Well, of course we all have values, we wouldn't steal off a child, we wouldn't hit an OAP, we love our families, we're conscientious at work, loyal to our friends... but they're just the tip of the iceberg. If we were to describe ourselves fully, what would all of our values be? And in relation to a guy too, because as nice as the guy is, if he doesn't get what we're about too, well...

Pete was making me wonder about my values and what made me a woman of high value in a man's eyes, or not. Plainly the woman in the negligee hadn't been high value, but the blonde was.

Why?

Here's an idea:

Values are what we would like to have or be, **standards** are how we demonstrate them and **principles** are what provide the guidelines for them. Now we can hold certain values internally but our way of life doesn't necessarily demonstrate them all the time, but they are there if someone digs around for them. Our standards reflect those values in the way we openly behave. Most people judge others by looking at their standards but they quite often don't actually find out until much later the principles they work on which determine both the values and the standards. Tricky stuff, huh? For example the blonde's standards demonstrated that she expected Pete to be persistent in calling her, patient about waiting, and acknowledge that she had other things going on in her life too. That indicated that the value she attributed to herself was high; that self-acknowledgement that she was worth waiting for, and that in turn suggested her principles. She placed herself above some guy trying to date her until he'd proved himself worth her attention. Now that was the reason for Peter attributing the comment 'high value' to her. I decided to think of a mnemonic to denote them by, since that was what I had always done when studying and this definitely felt like going back to school, and already being surprised at what I was learning.

     Values   V

     Standards S

     Principles P

 What could I attribute to them? Well Pete had called the blonde 'hot' too – he found her high value exciting and very appealing. OK, in that case **VSP** made her a **Very Sexy Person:** a brilliant start. That's what I wanted to be too.

 Of course there are all sorts of values we might have in relation to ourselves, but more importantly when looking for that elusive perfect guy to 'get', in relation to them. If their values don't coincide with ours, how well would that work, even if they appear to be the best thing since Clooney on toast?

 A little bit of 'collaboration theory' here: ***When the values and models of the world in two people align, then they can work together.***

 Now I'd been working from my own, very feminine, viewpoint, but it occurred to me early on that all of these principles applied equally to a man looking for the right woman. If I was looking for a VSP, so was he - otherwise I wouldn't be interested in him in the first place. Pete had already made it very clear that the high value/VSP angle was important for him too.

So:
- How do we value our family ties - high, medium or low? And is our potential date a budding Daddy or a confirmed Romeo?
- How do we value cleanliness, tidiness, presentational qualities? And is our potential date fashionable or a tramp?
- How do we value their involvement with our friends? And do we want our potential date to fit in or hold off?
- How do we want them to respond to our working commitments or career - accept it, support it or try to encourage us away from it - especially if you are a budding workaholic?
- What about politeness?
- Courtesy?
- Honesty?
- Commitment?
- Attention to you?
- Hobbies?
- Time spent away from each other?
- Travel?
- Homes?
- Finance?
- Shared activities?
- Children?

WOW the list could just go on and on. I started to wonder exactly what qualities - VALUES - I thought would be important in my perfect guy. My head started to reel with the sheer number of permutations there might be.

For example:

Principle	Value	Standard	How it may be demonstrated
I value honesty and openness.	Being honest in my dealings.	Always demonstrating this to me and the other people he deals with.	- Being frank. - Being open. - Including me in your social and family life (no separate life syndrome). - Never putting me off with an excuse. - No sneaky internet dating or 'friends'. - Telling me the truth even if it's awkward.
My family is important to me.	Family life.	Supporting my closeness with my family.	- Understanding I have to have time for my family. - Being polite and interacting with my family even if he's not that keen on them.

			- Respecting my family values.
- Not criticising or picking holes in my family.
- Inviting me to be involved in his family.
- Values his family.
- Makes time for his family and is supportive of them.
I enjoy my hobbies.	Engaging in hobbies.	Time to do what I enjoy doing.	- Accepting that I enjoy my hobbies and need time to do them.
- Maybe joining in with them if they interest him too.
- Encouraging me with whatever I'm doing.

| | | | - Appreciating what I'm doing – the skills, commitment, talent etc.
- Not making me feel guilty if I spend time on my hobbies – no 'I don't mind, really...' |
| --- | --- | --- | --- |
| Positivity. | Being positive about things. | How I approach life in general. | - Being generally positive about life.
- High energy.
- Optimistic and enthusiastic.
- Refuses to be beaten.
- Not depressive or easily gives up.
- Looks for the best solutions. |
| Loyalty. | Being loyal to people. | How I treat people. | - Only one relationship at a time. |

				<ul><li>No sly dating.</li><li>Supporting friends, family and partners.</li><li>Not being underhand.</li><li>Not gossiping about people.</li><li>Keeps promises.</li><li>Doesn't flirt with other people.</li></ul>

And there are many more things I could write in there too, depending on what I was addressing. Now, whatever I included in there for my values didn't necessarily need to be demonstrated all the time by the guy; or if it was a guy out looking, the woman. Maybe they weren't in the right situation to be able to demonstrate them. For example, with family values: I may have close family but he doesn't. It's hard to demonstrate a belief in something that you've no experience of because it is the role models you've had to follow that influence you and enable you to emulate them. He wouldn't be able to demonstrate being close to his family and spending time with them because they wouldn't be there to do that with - but he could demonstrate his support of me doing that with mine, and being keen to join in with mine...

Characteristics of people are surface level representations of people values. They may not be particularly good at something but their willingness to tackle it or do it indicates the value underpinning the attempt.

So, now even trickier - what if we don't always demonstrate those values in our standards? Standards are the compass to the way we live our values in our lives. They are not always related specifically to one set of actions, but are the way we tackle things generally. They may be high and obvious, low and undefined, or changeable. I decided what I was looking for was someone who knew the level of their standards, and stuck to them. Even if someone failed in their standards, the intention or attempt to improve themselves in line with their standards would display someone who was trying to get it right. If that person knew what your standards were and was trying to live up to them, they would be worth encouragement. Sometimes, maybe even just making it clear what our standards are can be enough to rapidly improve a blossoming relationship. I decided I would have to think about how to do that later on, but getting back to demonstrating standards, thinking about one of the most defining moments of my life made me start to understand this better.

One of my best remembered moments was of panic, paragliding in Turkey on my first singles holiday. I literally did climb a mountain that day - 6500 feet of one! Most of my fellow hotel companions had spent the week anticipating it - the climax of a week's spree of free love for them, and open mouthed amazement for me, observing from my 'I'm only just single...'place on the fence. Sweating anxiously, but determined not to be labelled both frigid **and** a wimp, I sat paralysed on the old bus, as we wound up the mountain, swinging round the corners like a slow moving rollercoaster, past the tourists and competition jump-points, to the international one, right at the summit. My stomach somersaulted, my heart pounded but I smiled nonchalantly (or so I hoped). The moment came to saddle up - literally because the flying suit worn had a 'seat' built into it so once attached to your 'pilot' - an experienced glider - and airborne, you could sit back into it and enjoy the ride . Oh really?

I looked down the slope, fully suited, saddled and scared shitless. One of my hotel companions was just ahead of me, ready to go. She turned, displaying a wonderfully ample saddle-derriere and said those immortal words, 'does my bum look big in this?' Laughter exploded, discharging my hysteria with it and knew I just had to do it. Within minutes I was running down the slope and into mid-air, thousands of feet above ground, with just the pilot and his parachute to get us safely back down. The descent was one of the most beautiful and awe-inspiring experiences of my life, purely because of the contrast between the sheer peace and silence up there compared to the hustle and bustle on our planet below. I am forever grateful I was coerced into it because it was such a defining moment. Courage, determination, self-belief - all finally pushed centre stage; caution and the ordinary banished to the wings - and all precipitated by the most inane comment I could imagine. No Shakespeare or Betjeman inspired quote for me - just sheer Carrie Bradshaw!

Ironically many of my epiphanies have been almost inconsequential moments in the midst of routine. Some profound - like realising the noises of everyday life still continued ignorantly around me as I sat for the minute's Remembrance Day silence in a coffee shop - how sad we so easily devalue the sacrifices made for us that we don't afford them one minute of tribute in the many millions we have for ourselves because of them. Or some ridiculous, like the conversation I now also remember I had with a narcissistic potential blind date. Informing me he was a part-time male model, and that he had abs like rocks, he went on to tell me how lucky I would be to date him because of his trim physique.

'…my waist is only 29 inches.'

'Wow, smaller than mine' I quipped back.

I expected him to laugh, but he didn't. I now see that a sense of humour and a sense of one's own humility are both important values for me too. He really believed he was doing me a favour. What about the favour I'm doing you by agreeing to this date, I wondered? People of value are the ones who listen to what **you** have to say too. The absurdity of the conversation made me see that.

Of course I don't jump off the side of mountains every day of my life, so maybe it would be difficult to demonstrate that particular somewhat 'gung-ho' attitude to life and new experiences in quite such an obviously dramatic way to most guys I met, but the essence of the values should show through in the way I approach life; head on, with determination and curiosity. I felt much better about myself when I thought about that experience. Yes, let's get on with this one then!

Life doesn't always make it easy to live in line with your internal values. You cannot always demonstrate them as we often live on two levels - our internal values and our behavioural values. Going back to the family values example - a guy's internal values might be very family-orientated; but if he has no close family it will be difficult for him to demonstrate that behaviourally in everyday life. That does not mean that he does not have the kind of values that would align with yours, but you will have to tease it out by demonstrating your values in that area and seeing how he reacts to them.

There is also another level of complexity involved here in that our values are often defined and determined by other role models in our lives - from childhood, from parents, from influential people in our lives at home, at work, in relationships. Sadly this is why there are some people who find it hard to trust if they've never had instances of situations where they've learned to do so in their lives. The guy who's been let down by an ex, or she's been unfaithful, will be anticipating unfaithfulness and may demonstrate that behaviourally by being unreliable himself as a defence mechanism. The guy who's never felt inclined to settle down before may seem like a committed bachelor to you. Women do it too – by stereotyping every man into the bad behaviour type they may have previously experienced in past relationships, or assuming every man is a player because they've had some dubious dates. Maybe these are not their internal values but they may be their demonstrated ones.

So how do you get to the internal values, and can the internal become the external values that are demonstrated by through standards too?

I gave myself two homily's here:

Don't fall in love with potential - what someone could be. Fall in love with what they are. And *leopards don't change their spots* - and this has remained a truism from many thousands of years ago; thank you Aristotle,

'we are what we repeatedly do…' (1)

Keeping up the 'road to love' analogy, standards are the compass by which we see the direction someone's values move in. Maybe if I describe standards as boundaries it helps put them into perspective. We all know that some things are ok and some things not, and somewhere in between the definitely ok and the definitely not there is a grey area. The definitely ok and the definitely not are the boundaries, and beyond or outside of them we would reject a persons' behaviour. It's like a slightly sick joke. There are some we laugh at - if slightly uncomfortably, saying - that's horrible!' and others we go quiet at, saying, 'that's sick!' There's the boundary. It's the same with standards. Somewhere between two boundaries of behavioural extremes, the standard behaviour will be ok for you. One step beyond, it's not.

What I was looking for was someone who both knew what their values and principles were, demonstrated them in their standards and those standards and values were sufficiently in alignment with my own for us to be compatible in the way we could live our lives together. Of course, I shouldn't forget that whatever I wish for in my guy, I had to be demonstrating also in my own values; fair's fair! I couldn't ask for him to be brave, good-humoured, fair-minded, family-orientated, kind, positive, determined, fun... if I wasn't. There is a law if attraction to everything in life. Maybe you don't stand naked under the stars, apart from a string of lucky charms, and burn a letter as you ask the universe for what you want and therefore immediately attract it to you - let's be realistic about this; but like does attract like. Remember a smile will generate a smile in return, a grumble a frown. Be careful what you wish for and only wish for the best for yourself.

So, the tricky bit to all of this is that whatever values and standards you are looking for and expecting to be demonstrated, you have to display yourself. This is part of the first rule of the strategy – the foundation, if you like: **if they don't coincide, you won't collide!**

Over to me then: If rule one of the strategy starts with looking at me, to make this easier I decided to make up a little 'look at me' test for myself. It's in the back of the book if you'd like to play the game on yourself, so you can value and de-value as many times as you like until you find the perfect mix! It works like this:

1. Examine yourself. What are YOUR values, and how do you demonstrate them in your standards of behaviour?

2. If there are standards there you don't like and which don't reflect your internal values, what are they? Are they learned patterns of behaviour from role models or past experience you think you could shift so they more closely reflect your real, internally held, values?
3. Make the shifts for yourself before you set about getting your guy - he's going to reflect the same values remember.
4. Now determine what the important values are for your guy, and how you expect them demonstrated in his behaviour and attitude.
5. Bingo - the kind of guy you're after... now get searching!

Funnily enough I did a mini version of this on Pete as he was talking about some more of his most dreadful dates. It was fascinating. There was the old age date, where the woman was photographed in sexy film star style HUGE sunglasses. Her details said she was 39. Pete commented that, despite her age, she must be hot from her style, so they met at a bar in Victoria. Or they were meant to but he looked all around the bar for about 20 minutes without seeing her and finally texting her.

'Where are you?'

She replied 'here, at the end of the bar.' He swung round to see a woman of about 55 in the same 'hot' sunglasses, perched around her wrinkles. Her first comment?

'I know what you're thinking - how old is she?'

His was:

'Do you want the diplomatic reply or the real one?'

She explained that no-one wanted to date a woman in her fifties. Probably Pete's polite reply should have been, 'a man in his fifties would' - a case of getting the right values (age related here). She rang her daughter to pick her up and when the daughter arrived, Pete commented, 'now I'd date your daughter...'

I wondered where I'd place that in the values box - for her, a lack of self-worth, honesty and also understanding of where she was in her life. For him, a lack of kindness and courtesy - and why just go on what looks 'hot'? It's not what we look like, is it? It's what we ARE like that matters.

And ironically there was one which he classed the best, where again he met a woman in a wine bar but this time she was 'hot' - in fact, he said, she was dressed to kill - 'easy tiger!' and the evening progressed well with him eventually going back to her place for coffee (again). This lady didn't appear in her negligee though, although they did progress further than the coffee and onto the necking. Pete hoped it would go further still but it didn't and she waved him off at about 3am with a copy of a DVD they'd been talking about and which she lent him. He was sure she would call him and arrange to meet up again so he could return the DVD. She didn't.

'So what went wrong there?' I asked, very curious as the DVD loan seemed to be the perfect set-up for a return visit.

'I've no idea, she just didn't reply,' he said sadly. 'Maybe she was just out to play - which is really unfair on a guy because I was being serious,' and his face took on a slightly peevish 'it's not fair' little boy expression, conveniently forgetting some of the other

stories he'd just told me with his standards very obviously pinned to them:
- 'I don't want to spend too much time dating monogamously as if it doesn't work out I will have been wasting my time…'
- 'Every date starts off as being a one night stand, but if it's good enough to be a one night stand, then maybe it can stretch to 2 or more…'
- 'We're all players playing the dating game; we just play it in different ways…'

No prizes for working out where Pete's values were starting to show themselves to be. All of a sudden they started to fit in with MY values rather less, no matter how 'hot' **he** looked as he smiled back at me at the end of the tale – deep brown eyes flashing with amusement, wide white-toothed smile, broad shoulders, delicious after-shave and smart style aside…

Chapter 3: Man-nav or Sat-girl - chose your weapons!

Pete's tale about the blonde demonstrated that there was a way she showed she was high value and made him keen to follow up on her. So how did she do that apart from the obvious valuing of herself so highly in what she'd said to him? I'd decided as my plan - my strategy, entailed me getting from A to B, where A was anonymous (to Pete) and B was, well, let's call it 'Blonde' as she was so obviously the goal for him, I must need some basic directions.

It actually doesn't matter what you call it - It's just about finding the route. So here we go with a handy hint and a mnemonic to spell it out (so glad I have spellcheck to help there too!):

R = your roadmap You wouldn't set out without one if you didn't know where you were going, would you? If you want to get somewhere, you need to know the route there. Let's work out the route to get the guy…

O = others The other people who help you get there. If you lose your way somewhere what do you do? Ask a policeman! Of course – although there aren't so many of those about on the streets now, so phone a friend instead! Prime your peers to encourage you to regularly achieve what you're setting out to do.

A = accountability You need to make yourself accountable for your actions and achieving your goal. Everything we do in life we do by our own efforts, so if finding the relationship of your dreams is an important goal, put as much effort into it as you would into anything else that had such importance. If you wanted a qualification, you would have to study for it, if you want to master a new skill you have to practice it. Make your efforts equal to the prize and put an equal amount of effort into getting your guy as the value you place on it.

D = direction And often that means having someone who can take you in the right direction to achieve your goal. That may be friends, a mentor, even the guys you meet along the way. They all have something to tell you and teach you; make the most of it.

So looking at the roadmap, one of the first things that occurred to me was that a journey always ends up with a destination. Mine was obviously to **get the guy,** but which guy, and where was he? What were the stops on the journey going to be? First of all where was I going to meet him? I was sitting in a pub with Pete. I looked around - was this a good place to meet my guy - or any guy to meet their girl? I was targeting Pete until now, but that wasn't being very successful so maybe I ought to be looking out for other candidates too.

The pub was filled with couples deep in conversation at tables for two or propped against the wall; a girl hugging her glass of wine or alcopop, a guy swigging away at his pint. At the bar the singles were ranged up, like the available goods on a shop shelf. Two women in tight, short skirts and too much make-up were leaving red lipstick rings at the top of their glasses. That would look good on a guy's cheek! Some men, deep in an animated conversation about last night's game, shoulders rounding as they huddled into their circle, shutting out the casual passer by - or single woman. They may be married guys down the pub escaping the missus anyway, but not very promising whatever. Beyond that there was an old guy sat on the bar stool at the end, eyes glued to the TV screen. He was about 60 and not my type (I am joking!). And that was it… Well, not here definitely. So where? Time to get the brain into gear again.

What linked all the people in the pub? What was their common denominator? Overall, I guessed it was generally 'unavailable' for a number of reasons - married, partnered, already dating, not interested, too old or unsuitable; unavailable in a word. This was obviously the wrong place for available guys and the same for girls. So what places were the right places? Bars and clubs where the singles went? Applying my values ideas I wondered what kind of singles they would turn out to be. I cast a quick glance at Pete still talking about one of his recent dates - probably the brunette - thinking, he always meets them in a wine bar or a club. That made it almost certainly a 'no' for me given the values I was starting to perceive in him.

All these people in this place were of specific types. If I was looking for a guy with specific values and attributes then maybe I needed to look in the kind of places he would frequent as a matter of course – ah, an epiphany! Define the guy by his values and then match the possible place to look for him to them too. I needed an A to Z - and not of London! So here we are with the definitive guide to places and values…

And just a tip on reading this - when anything is in *italics* it means here's an opportunity you could have any time of the day without even trying! More on what I call double or quits later on…

Alphabet	Places	Likely values/attributes
A	*Art gallery*	cultural
B	Book club	Cultural
	Bars	Lively, social, party animal
	Business networking	Career orientated, professional
	Beach	Social, sporty
	Bowling	Sporty but light hearted
	Bingo	Less active
	Barbecues	Social and outdoorsy
C	Cycling club	Sporty, specific interest
	Coffee shop	Social
	Comic book club	Specific interests
	Comedy club	Light hearted and social
	Ceroc	Loves dancing
	Clubs (see bars)	Lively, social, party animal
	Conventions for hobbies/interests	Specific interests
	Conferences	Career orientated, professional, Specific interests
	Cocktail bars	Social, lively, party animal
	Classes	Personal growth orientated, and specific interest
	Car boot sales	Practical, material, sociable
D	*Dog walking*	Loves dogs, walking, outdoorsy, sociable
	Dance classes – all sorts	Loves dancing, sociable, active
	Debating clubs	Cultural, intellectual, articulate, social, confident
E	Exercise classes	Specific interest, sporty, looks after self
	Edinburgh Fringe	Sense of humour, unusual, cultural
	Elevator (lift)	Sociable
	Exhibitions	Cultural, intellectual

	Electronics store – eg Apple	Geeky, but very male
	Evening classes	Self growth, specific interest
F	Folk club	Specific musical interest
	Fairs (misc types eg mystic, steam etc)	Specific interests
	Festivals	Specific interests, and often music lovers – various
	Football matches	The obvious one for 1000s of men!
	Flower markets	Social, specific interests
	(through) Friends	Social – and anything is possible!
G	*Gym*	Sporty, looks after self
	Golf	Specific interest
	Gardens	Specific interest
	Garden centres	Specific interest
H	Health club	Sporty, looks after self
	Horse riding	Specific interest
	Health food shop	Specific interest
	Hotel foyers and bars- or any foyers	Sociable
I	*Internet*	Anything is possible but read 'Are you the one?' first!
	Ikea	Sociable
	Ice skating	Specific interest, sporty, sociable, fun
J	Jive dancing	Loves dancing and sociable
	Jazz clubs	Sociable and specific interest
K	Kick Boxing	Male orientated, sporty
	Kayaking	Sporty, specific interest
	Karaoke bars	Sociable, extrovert, maybe an exhibitionist
L	Line dancing	Specific interest
	Library	Self -growth, love reading, intellectual, cultural

	Lido	Swimming, social
	Lectures	Self-growth, specific interest, intellectual, cultural
M	*Museums*	Self-growth, specific interest, intellectual, cultural
	Meet-up groups	Social – anything could be involved
	markets	social
N	*Night clubs*	Social, lively, party animal
	Night school	Self-growth, specific interest, intellectual, cultural
	Neighbours	Who knows – anything could happen!
O	Opera	Intellectual, cultural, music lover
P	*Pubs*	Social, lively,
	Parties	Social lively, party animal
	Public speaking groups	Self-growth, specific interest, intellectual, cultural
	Parks	Outdoorsy, social
	Public lectures	Self-growth, specific interest, intellectual, cultural
	Photography club	Specific interest
Q	Quiz night	Quiz night, likes challenges, social
	Queues	Social – anything could happen
R	Restaurants	Social, lively food lover
	Races	Likes a flutter and an occasion, specific interest, social
	Record shops	Social and music lover
	Rowing clubs	Specific interest and sporty
	Rugby	Specific interest and sporty
S	Salsa	Loves dancing, social
	Supermarkets	Social – anything could happen
	Shopping	Social – anything could happen
	Sailing	Specific interest

	Speed dating	Social, lively and anything could happen
	Secret cinema club	Specific interest
	Specialist conventions (eg are you a trekkie?)	Specific interest
T	Tennis club	Specific interest and sporty
	Toastmaster groups	Self-growth, intellectual, social
U	*University*	Self-growth, intellectual, social
	Underbelly festival	Self-growth, intellectual, social
	Urban golf	Specific interest, sporty, social
V	Volunteering	Self-growth, intellectual, social, a giver
	Volley ball (on the beach)	Social, sporty
W	Walking clubs	Enjoys walking, sporty, social
	Writers groups	Intellectual, specific interest, cultural
	Wine tasting groups	Specific interest, social
	Whisky tasting class	Specific interest, social, Scottish
	Wine bars	Social, lively, party animal
	Waterstones	Enjoys reading, intellectual, cultural, specific interests
	Watersports	Specific interest, sporty
X	Xtreme sports clubs	Specific interest, mad
Y	Yoga – Bikram or Ashtanger best	Self-growth, looks after self
	Yachting	Specific interest, sporty
	Laughter yoga	Self-growth, looks after self, social
Z	Zoo lates – at Zoos in London from 2012	Loves animals, specific interest

Now, none of these places are specific - the address of a venue. They are generic because the options and possibilities where you live will be different and specific to where you live. And it isn't an exhaustive list by any means - think of all the different subjects you could take at evening classes or the topics you could go to discuss at a debating club, or hear a lecture about. Think of all the different types of sport you could be interested in or hobbies you may have. From astronomy to Zen Buddhism, aardvargs to Zoroastroism, archery to yoga (don't quibble, it's almost a 'Z'), there are thousands of different angles to follow up. But what it does show you is that there are many, many places to look for a guy (or girl), depending on what they're interested in and what their values dictate their behaviour to be in terms of standards. How would you determine which to target then?

Well let's try it out:

Your values:

- Loves animals.
- Sociable and friendly but not a party animal.
- A bit of a traditionalist and perhaps a little shy.
- Intellectual and culturally interested.
- Into self- growth.
- Positive.
- Career orientated.
- Has specific sporting interests – eg is a golfer and sailor.
- Likes reading.

What might this guy's pattern of life be, identifying everything he might be involved in as a result? All the likely places are highlighted in bold. Of course that doesn't mean that he WILL be at any of them but the chances of him being at any of those kinds of places is significantly higher than the various bars and clubs which we immediately assume we should go to and then find the type of guy we are looking for isn't there.

Alphabet	Places	Likely values/attributes
A	*Art gallery*	Cultural
B	**Book club**	Cultural
	Bars	Lively, social, party animal
	Business networking	Career orientated, professional
	Beach	Social, sporty
	Bowling	Sporty but light hearted
	Bingo	Less active
	Barbecues	Social and outdoorsy
C	Cycling club	Sporty, specific interest
	Coffee shop	Social
	Comic book club	Specific interests
	Comedy club	Light hearted and social
	Ceroc	Loves dancing
	Clubs (see bars)	Lively, social, party animal
	Conventions for hobbies/interests	Specific interests
	Conferences	Career orientated, professional, Specific interests
	Cocktail bars	Social, lively, party animal
	Classes	Personal growth orientated, and specific interest
	Car boot sales	Practical, material, sociable
D	*Dog walking*	Loves dogs, walking, outdoorsy, sociable
	Dance classes – all sorts	Loves dancing, sociable, active
	Debating clubs	Cultural, intellectual, articulate, social, confident
E	Exercise classes	Specific interest, sporty, looks after self
	Edinburgh Fringe	
	Elevator (lift)	Sense of humour, unusual, cultural
	Exhibitions	

	Electronics store – eg Apple	Sociable Cultural, intellectual Geeky, but very male
	Evening classes	Self growth, specific interest
F	Folk club	Specific musical interest
	Fairs (misc types eg mystic, steam etc)	Specific interests
	Festivals	Specific interests, and often music lovers – various
	Football matches	The obvious one for 1000s of men!
	Flower markets	Social, specific interests
	(through) Friends	Social – and anything is possible!
G	*Gym*	Sporty, looks after self
	Golf	**Specific interest**
	Gardens	Specific interest
	Garden centres	Specific interest
H	Health club	Sporty, looks after self
	Horse riding	Specific interest
	Health food shop	Specific interest
	Hotel foyers and bars – or any foyers	**Sociable**
I	*Internet*	Anything is possible but read 'Are you the one?' first!
	Ikea	Sociable
	Ice skating	Specific interest, sporty, sociable, fun
J	Jive dancing	Loves dancing and sociable
	Jazz clubs	Sociable and specific interest
K	Kick Boxing	Male orientated, sporty
	Kayaking	Sporty, specific interest
	Karaoke bars	Sociable, extrovert, maybe an exhibitionist

L	Line dancing	Specific interest
	Library	**Self-growth, love reading, intellectual, cultural**
	Lido	Swimming, social
	Lectures	**Self-growth, specific interest, intellectual, cultural**
M	***Museums***	**Self-growth, specific interest, intellectual, cultural**
	Meet-up groups	**Social – anything could be involved**
	markets	social
N	*Night clubs*	Social, lively, party animal
	Night school	**Self-growth, specific interest, intellectual, cultural**
	Neighbours	**Who knows – anything could happen!**
O	**Opera**	Intellectual, cultural, music lover
P	*Pubs*	Social, lively,
	Parties	**Social lively, party animal**
	Public speaking groups	**Self-growth, specific interest, intellectual, cultural**
	Parks	Outdoorsy, social
	Public lectures	**Self-growth, specific interest, intellectual, cultural**
	Photography club	Specific interest
Q	Quiz night	Quiz night, likes challenges, social
	Queues	Social – anything could happen
R	*Restaurants*	Social, lively food lover
	Races	Likes a flutter and an occasion, specific interest, social
	Record shops	Social and music lover
	Rowing clubs	Specific interest and sporty
	Rugby	Specific interest and sporty

S	Salsa	Loves dancing, social
	Supermarkets	Social – anything could happen
	Shopping	Social – anything could happen
	Sailing	**Specific interest**
	Speed dating	Social, lively and anything could happen
	Secret cinema club	Specific interest
	Specialist conventions (eg are you a trekkie?)	Specific interest
T	Tennis club	Specific interest and sporty
	Toastmaster groups	Self-growth, intellectual, social
U	*University*	**Self-growth, intellectual, social**
	Underbelly festival	Self-growth, intellectual, social
	Urban golf	Specific interest, sporty, social
V	Volunteering	Self-growth, intellectual, social, a giver
	Volley ball (on the beach)	Social, sporty
W	Walking clubs	Enjoys walking, sporty, social
	Writers groups	**Intellectual, specific interest, cultural**
	Wine tasting groups	Specific interest, social
	Whisky tasting class	Specific interest, social, Scottish
	Wine bars	Social, lively, party animal
	Waterstones	Enjoys reading, intellectual, cultural, specific interests
	Watersports	Specific Interest, sporty
X	Xtreme sports clubs	Specific interest, mad
Y	**Yoga – Bikram or Ashtanger best**	Self-growth, looks after self
	Yachting	**Specific interest, sporty**
	Laughter yoga	Self-growth, looks after self, social
Z	**Zoo lates – at Zoos in London from 2012**	**Loves animals, specific interest**

37

I suddenly realised exactly how many chances there were to find more of the right guys without wasting time going to the places he WON'T be. But what about all those situations and places that are in italics - and what is this double or quits time idea?

Double or quits:

So of course I could employ this strategy to go out looking for a guy to meet every day for most of the day, and no doubt that would be very effective after a period of time, but whilst I was doing that what would happen to all the other things I do, like working, spending time with friends - or are essential; sleeping, eating and so on? I pictured all the forgone curries and cocktails with the girls, or nights curled up with a good book or a DVD, and whilst forgoing the curries and cocktails might do wonders for my figure, it would also make me a sad single desperate for a guy. Would that be the right route to my destination? Oops, no! Not desperate by any means. Pete was still talking about the blonde. How much more could he find to say about her, I wondered? My eye roved around the pub whilst my mind roved around the problem. Then I got it - of course, just because you were doing things OTHER than seeking out the right guy, it didn't mean that you couldn't still be idly looking for the guy at the same time - after all, we're women, right? We multi-task! (Guys – it's time to learn that skill too).

Life cannot revolve around just one thing, there has to be balance, with the goal of finding what you want in a reasonable way: so let's set another sub-strategy here. First of all decide how much time you are going to devote to finding this right guy or girl, and then allocate it around what you do. If it is 100% important for you to have that special relationship with that special one, then devote 100% of your time to it whilst multi-tasking working, eating, sleeping, shopping (almost forgot that) and seeing friends, following hobbies and so on. You can achieve that simply by using the double or quits strategy:

Double or…:

I remembered how I'd walked into the class I was going to teach my students a few weeks before. It was all about being observant, and here's the little test I'd set…

The test?
　Where is the waste paper bin in the room? *(Next to me, at the front).*
　What is the number on the lecture room door? *(325).*
　What colour is the door to the entrance of the building? *(Green).*
　Where is the nearest bench outside? *(Right by the entrance door).*
　Where is the fire evacuation instruction posted up? *(Notice board in the corridor they walk through to get to the lecture room).*

Most of them scored 1 out of 5 - they noticed the waste paper bin because I was standing beside it; or zero, because it was too early on the morning to even focus! How unobservant are we?

Well, actually we are very observant, but we need to be focussed to make use of what we observe. If I had pre-warned my students there was going to be a test on what they saw as they came to class that day, and that it would give them 50% of the exam results for their qualification, they would have got 5 out of 5. But as it was they weren't focussed - or even looking.

So what happens when you are looking AND focussed? BINGO! We see most of what is going around us in a subconsciously noticing kind of way but disregard 90% of it and the remaining 10% of it is directly influenced by our current internal focus. So now is the time to switch focus. Look for any 'indicator' that a guy may respond to you to enable you to start communicating with him. Any relationship is born out of communication and our easiest form of communication is to talk to someone... Whenever doing ANYTHING, look for the slightest opportunity to react to an 'indicator' of interest, for example:

- Smile back to any 'after you'; give away a smile in the shopping or ATM queue; start a conversation.
- Comment on a book or newspaper or magazine a guy is reading, and start a conversation.
- In any queue - any comment will do to start a conversation.
- Compliment a guy in passing; 'I like your tie', or 'that's a nice smile' - any compliment is a welcome one, and then start a conversation.
- Pick a daily reason to say something to a guy - for example, anyone wearing red - and start a conversation

- Smile at every guy you meet, whether he's young, old, hot or hellish - it's noticeable if you're a happy person and other people want to approach you.

NB – for every time I say 'guy', swop for 'girl' if you're a guy, of course!

Now an indicator doesn't have to be a smile or a look or any obvious positive interest in you. This guy doesn't know you from Adam. Unless you are a stunning beauty, he may not even look your way unless you attract his attention somehow. After all, his focus is probably as bad as yours was and he's noticing 90% of things subconsciously WITHOUT realising that he's only noticed 10% of what's going on around him - AND that 10% will be based around what he's focussed on. If he's focussed on his new car, or completing that report at work, is he looking out for an amazing new date? No. Get working, girl!

We all know that practice makes perfect and it is easy to forget something unless we practice it. So here are where the daily rituals come in to remind you of your focus. I don't mean a mantra, 'I must get the guy, I must get the guy… or I must talk to a guy today, I must talk to a guy today...' but a series of things you can do as part of your regular routine so that eventually they become second nature to you. They are all designed to make you more approachable, more proactive, more opportunistic, more focussed, and therefore more attractive to a guy. Looking for the indicators is an example of a set of rituals, so it's 'simples'! Make up your own:

I'll smile and start a conversation if:

- He's wearing red.
- He smiles at me.
- He pats a dog.
- He reads a newspaper or a book.
- He's in the queue with me.
- He orders latte.
- He's tall.
- He's short.
- He doesn't smile at me.
- He's wearing…

The list is endless and so are the opportunities to talk. Multi-task it, girl.

…or quits:

Nobody likes a quitter, so don't. If you don't get a good reaction, smile and move on. How many men are there in this world (or guys – how many girls)?

The beauty of this strategy is that you can simply be living your normal life yet still pro-actively seeking out that perfect person. Of course if you are going to the places and doing the things that are demonstrative of the values you want to find in your perfect partner, then all the better. A mathematician would be able to calculate the improved odds from doing so - I wondered if my phone had an app on it to do that too, but I couldn't whip it out in front of Pete and start calculating. He was some kind of financial whizz, so he said, so I suppose I could have asked him, but I didn't think that was such a good idea as the brunette from the previous week had regressed back to the blonde. I did let an idly curious thought stray into words.

'Pete, how would you describe your perfect woman? Is it looks or something else?'

He stopped in mid-flow and looked at me in surprise, as if he assumed he'd already made that clear.

'Why do you ask?'

'Well, you are talking a lot about the hot blonde and the hot brunette – what makes them 'hot' for you?'

'Hmm, well, obviously looks count, but it's the value they place on themselves, and the energy type they project too.'

'Energy type?' I was actually already getting the picture but I wanted him to just clarify before moving on to the next part of my plan.

'Yes, energy type. You see…' he settled more comfortably on the bar stool and I knew I was about to get a lecture, but maybe this one would be more interesting and useful than the hot blonde/brunette one. 'A person's energy level shows what kind of person they are. If they are positive and lively and friendly, then they are attractive - you know they would be fun to be with. If they project an independent kind of approach - plenty of interests, definite career goals, friends they do things with, family they rate as important, then they seem well rounded and you don't worry that if you got into a relationship with them they'd be clingy and needy. You wouldn't be smothered.'

I smiled at him. 'Is it nice if a woman approaches you and smiles then, and talks without you having to approach her?'

'Definitely. And actually, unless she's really hot I probably wouldn't notice her, or approach her anyway - I'd feel kinda awkward.' I gave him a double-take 'kinda' look back. Coy didn't actually seem his style, but then maybe there are hidden depths to everyone that we don't plumb until we get to know them better.

'Out of interest, did **you** approach the hot blonde or the hot brunette then?'

'Oh no, the brunette asked me to pass her drink to her at the bar and then told me I was sweet, and the blonde sat next to me on the tube and commented on the article I was reading in the paper.'

Job done: and strategy proven; now let's get cracking!

Chapter 4: Single to social in simple steps - and here come the guys!

I was all fired up with my amazing ideas by the time the evening ended with Pete. Surprisingly enough he suggested we go out again sometime and whilst I guessed he wasn't interested in me like he was the hot blonde or the hot brunette, his observations about men's views of women and what made them were surprisingly useful, so I said yes politely and agreed that he could ring me sometime. I actually didn't really expect another phone call at all and settled down to think about a few other road blocks that had cropped up on the route to success.

It's all very well talking about deciding on your standards and values, and going out to all these different places on the Man-nav, and Sat-girl and approaching all these strangers with the aim of turning them into potential relationships, but what if you are unsure and shy? And ironically, although I was setting out my strategy for me - a girl - what about if you're a guy and trying to do the same thing? We hit a major roadblock straightaway because no matter how proactive the girl is, the guy has to be prepared to respond. Now that is not so 'simples'. Maybe I needed to factor in a strategy for guys too? Let's start with the basics then, because sitting there in that pub and looking around me, I knew that I wasn't a go-get-em-girl. I was, in fact, often a bit of a wallflower and that was one of the reasons Pete hadn't been that interested in me to start with. I also was having a tricky time deciding which standards and values were most important and where there were shades of grey (not fifty though), as I'd never done this before. It was like re-discovering me! I went home that night with my head buzzing with questions and theories and confusion, so I settled down the next day with a big bar of chocolate and a cappuccino to THINK. This is what I thought...

Just like building a house to live in, I needed to check the foundations to it; me - and what I did. Then when I knew they were firm and decided, I could apply my strategy and deploy at will - no man would be safe from me ever again!

So here we go:

Step 1: Hello, I'm...

Hello. Who am I? That sounds like a silly question. Of course I know who I am - I don't need a label like I have at work team building meetings, surely?' Of course not, we all know who we think we are, but if we weren't looking out through our own eyes, what would the person be like that we are looking at? The person other people see is sometimes very different to the one we think we are. We know how we feel inside about things. We remember things that have happened to us and these have created our catalogue of experience, and therefore also our response to anything we encounter in the future. Sometimes those responses have become so ingrained in the neural pathways that regular repetition has created in our brains, we aren't even aware we make time. We don't even notice. Someone else does though. They look at you with objective eyes every day and see all your routines, your repetitions and your habitual behaviour, good or bad. And people react to people. Response gets response. Bad response often gets bad response, and good response quite often gets good response. We want a good response from the people we meet to that 'hello, I'm…' so that means you have to be able to look through those other peoples' eyes and see you as they see you – a tricky, and uncomfortable thing to do.

How are you going to see yourself the way others do? Here's my way. Looking at yourself, your routines, your behaviours, your reactions to different situations, the way you feel about and in different situations, what you like/dislike and what you want to achieve for yourself - work out first exactly who you think you are, and then try it from someone else's angle.

- Describe yourself the way you see yourself (aren't you gorgeous!)
- Describe yourself the way you think your friends see you (a big question mark here - dohhh!)
- Ask a friend to describe you – (light bulb moment)

How do they differ?

Put the three together - this is you inside and out - the way you see yourself and also the way the world sees you. Hmm - well that's maybe a little different to the way **I** saw me!

Sometimes the composite answer is surprising, maybe even shocking. Perhaps you didn't realise you did that annoying thing all the time, or maybe you didn't realise that someone else sees your internal character as quite different to you. I was recently completely taken aback by someone saying I was a very calm and meditative person – in fact they assumed I must meditate to achieve such a chilled attitude in the face of all adversities. I looked behind me to see who it was they were addressing these comments to – but *'Oh, ok! It's me!'*

Well, that's very odd because I always feel like I'm rushing everywhere, trying not to drop one of the various sets of balls I have permanently in the air - but of course that's the me I know inside. The outward me seems to apparently calmly rotate those balls without so much as a flicker of hesitation. Hmm, again - how interesting for me!

Now, what do you like and what do you dislike about this you you've just met? Write it as two lists with a separate column next to both lists, and then comment on the likes/dislikes...

I like about me…	I dislike about me…	What can I do with this?	How can I change this?
Friendly.	Bad timekeeping.		
My organised approach to work.	My tendency to fritter money on things I don't really need (clothes).		
I'm fair-minded.	My weight – too much.		
I'm helpful, and I always have time for my friends no matter how busy I am.	I don't always share my ideas because I'm not sure if they're right/good or not.		

So now you have a description of you – *'ooh, that's a bit surprising…!'* and have also pinpointed the things you want to capitalise on and promote. Use them to promote yourself, and the things you don't like and want to lose; examine or change.

Step 2 – drawing up the change plan

So now you say, OK – what am I meant to do with all this STUFF? I've pulled myself apart into little pieces, what am I meant to do with the pieces? Well, now put them all back together like a jigsaw puzzle, but this time focussing on the good bits and watering down, changing or getting rid of the bad bits.

For example, you think you are a kind person - and your friends all agree. How can you make sure that a stranger meeting you straightaway also recognises kindness in you and your attitude? Is it through the way you speak to them, approach them, your body language, what you offer to do, how much time you spend with them, or the interest you take in them, as opposed to talking about yourself? Once you've identified some of the specific things you say, do or demonstrate in your behaviour; that are the specific qualities of you, you can set about promoting them more or downsizing their importance in the way people perceive you, and hey presto! A slightly different person starts to emerge - one who you like and **want** to be seen as.

Similarly for the things you don't like about yourself, you can think around ways of changing or banishing them. Say, although you are full of bright ideas, you lack the confidence in yourself to be prepared to put them forward. Consequently someone else - at work or with friends - always comes up with the great idea and is applauded for it. You stand back, thinking in irritation, *'but that was MY idea…'* and after a few times, the irritation becomes a little bit of resentment - *'why does everyone else always get the pat on the back, or be in the limelight, or get called amazing fun for their great ideas...'* and then your demeanour may take on a sulky tone, or you stand back even more, thinking there's no point because your great ideas never get noticed. All of a sudden you've sunk into frustration, anger and disillusionment - and everyone thinks - *'they're a little touchy/negative... I'll watch what I say to them...'* and isolation starts to creep in.

Which is better?

To promote the positives: or wallow in the negatives?

Of course it is the positive approach in all things that gets the best response, and that is exactly what this plan is going to help you do - promote the positives in you to achieve a positive outcome - from solo to sociable; alone to with friends.

Now, having created your lists of likes and dislikes, you need to take each one individually and examine it. And each time you do, you will end up with a number of ideas about what you could do with, or about, your likes or dislikes. It may look something like this:

I like about me…	What can I do with this?	I dislike about me…	How can I change this?
My friendly smile.	Make a conscious effort to always smile at everyone I meet - not a big cheesy grin, but a little smile of greeting.	My bad timekeeping.	Set my watch and clocks five minutes fast to make me set out a little earlier, work out when I know I have to be somewhere on time, how long it will take to get there, park or find the place, and consider what the possible delays could be – add more time on for these.
My organised approach to work.	Keep it going - and extend it to doing the house work, doing the household finances,	My tendency to fritter money on things I don't really need (clothes).	If I don't want to spend money when I'm out - take a limited amount of cash with me, and leave my credit cards at home. I can't spend more

	keeping in touch with friends and family, not forgetting birthday cards or that thing that was meant to go on the shopping list... If you have a skill in one area of your life, you can easily also apply it to another area of your life and successfully improve that area for yourself too.		than I've got. Or, if I'm going to get something specific, do some research first so I know where I can get it cheapest, and then stick to that one thing only. Or, plan a rewards for myself on getting home without spending when I didn't intend to (not something you're going to spend money on - of course!) Little treats like having some chocolate watching that TV instead of doing the housework, ringing one of your new friends to boast...
I'm fair-minded.		My weight - too much.	I'm going to choose a diet and exercise plan, set myself a

				target weight and a time to get to it, and my reward will be to spend some money on a dress or something that shows off exactly how gorgeous I've become!
I'm helpful, and I always have time for my friends no matter how busy I am.			I don't always share my ideas because I'm not sure if they're right/good or not.	

You get the picture? I'm not going to show you mine - far too embarrassing!

When you've worked your way through the list, you'll be left with some things you just want to scrap, and stop doing forever, some you can change a little and then they become positive, and some things that are already positive and you've just found ways of doing them more and more and more... And ultimately what this will do for you, as you work at them, following your **'hello I'm...'** plan, is to make yourself more interesting, more skilled, more likeable, more popular and more happy within.

And more YOU!

Happiness within really shows; it shines out from your eyes, your demeanour, your response and the way you approach life in general, like an internal beacon, saying *'hello, I'm good to know - come and meet me.'*

Step 3 - how to talk yourself up, not down

We all have those little moments when we question ourselves; how clever we are, nice we are, attractive we are, and fun we are. Even the most confident of us have them. I was having quite a lot of those as I listened to Pete, but what he said about the high value woman made me realise I had to find a way of talking myself **up** to valuing myself highly rather than **down** to valuing myself little, because no-one else was going to do it for me.

It is very easy to talk yourself out of things or to talk yourself down, and it's born out of your own insecurity. Oh dear, a bit of a catch 22 there, then - and also, from your past experience and role models. Look at it this way, if you're used to someone telling you you're not good enough then after a while you start to believe it. It's all about debunking that belief and setting up a fresh belief for yourself - that you are good enough. How could I do that? Little by little...

Ask yourself these questions:
- Why do you think you're not good enough/can't do it?
- Who has told you that in the past?

- Were they jealous or in competition with you - or even just wanted to have the upper hand *in some way?*
- Were they right or did you prove them wrong?
- Who else do you know who regularly overcomes obstacles and difficulties?
- How do they do it?
- When where the times I **were** right/good enough?

Very often the people who tell us we aren't good enough, can't do it, shouldn't do it or are struggling with their own self-limiting beliefs. If they transfer them onto us and see us failing or not trying, it makes them feel better about themselves. Now that doesn't make them a mean person, it just means it's a little like climbing the greasy pole; you tread on someone below you in order to get higher up it yourself. The greasy pole here is self-esteem. Those self-limiting beliefs can come from parents - an easy way to keep their children in check as they become more challenging and independent when they are growing up, or from ex-partners trying to hold onto you when they sense you slipping out of their control, or competition - the reason there is obvious, or simply from someone who is struggling with their own demons and sees you as an easy target.

We also regularly let our past bad experiences limit our confidence in the future. If you've had a partner who cheated, you wonder if the next one will. If you had a manipulative partner, you'll be wary of who gets close next time. If you've dated a gold-digger, you'll be watching your wallet - yes this all applies to guys too!

The answer to all of this is that you are only limited by what you believe you are limited by. You are good enough, and you can try anything you like. Even if you fail or wish you'd done better, each mistake you make is an opportunity to learn and every time you mess up you're better at NOT messing up the next time. Pete told me some interesting date stories on this topic which illustrated for me how you're seen if you are a giver-upper.

The first one I felt really sorry for. She met him in a bar for a drink (again) and was so nervous she could hardly speak. Guess what? Despite being very pretty, there was never a second date. If you're so nervous you can't communicate normally, how can you build a relationship with anyone? If you've even got to a first date stage with someone they're obviously open to finding out more about you, so you're good enough already.

The next one was so naïve she assumed that because there was a first date they were made for life, and then proceeded to down three very large glasses of wine straightaway and then tell him her life story. She had a few of my strategy ideas in place - she told Pete that she would expect flowers from him every time she saw him and of course that 'being exclusive ' would now be a pre-requisite to seeing him again- so she set her standards stall out from the start, but his response? 'You only get flowers if you deserve them.' Why?

'Well, it devalued the flowers didn't it?' He explained to me.

I laughed quite ruefully at that as I remembered the guy who'd done a similar thing to me once. After 3 dates he'd asked me what he should call me. 'Well, my name would be ok I think' I said smartly before he went on to explain he meant should he refer to me as a *friend* or a *girlfriend?* I jokingly replied that if he wanted to call me a girlfriend then he could - I was a girl after all - but don't expect me to call him my *boyfriend*. I thought that was it but then when I didn't immediately consent to another date, the messages started, asking when I had more time to see him etc. He understood if I was busy at work or with other things in my life, but he so missed seeing me and hearing my voice that he would wait for me as long as it took, because *if we weather this storm then we will be so much stronger for it.* At this stage I did exactly the same as Pete did, and backed off very hurriedly, feeling suffocated by the pressure that this guy was putting on me. It said 'needy' all over it and obviously came from his self-limiting beliefs - that he had to hang onto me as tight as he could in order to keep me. In fact it caused the reverse to happen as I ran for the hills.

Sadly our past experiences do sometimes make us needy at times if they have been bad or disappointing, but we have to work hard to get past them. They are not set in stone and remember this:

'Our lives are defined by opportunities, including the ones we miss.' (2)

Step 4 - starting to be social

Ah, another tricky one.

Where to go and what to do:

Start with what is easy for you, and doesn't entail walking in, and announcing yourself to the world:
- Join a class.
- Join a club.
- Volunteer to help out at something you think important.
- Enlist a friend to go somewhere new with you as moral support.
- Smile at whoever you meet.
- Say yes to all invitations to events or social meetings.
- Start a ritual (remember those from chapter 3?) to talk to one new person a day wherever you are. The more you do it, the more instinctive it will become.
- Make yourself a social hub - hold a 'happy-hour' get together regularly, invite everyone along to it - at a local bar or pub, or convenient meeting point. Ask friends and colleagues to bring friends and colleagues and a watch your network grow.

And last of all, whatever you do or wherever you go:
- Go out somewhere! No-one ever meets someone new in their own home.

This way, even if Mr or Ms Right doesn't automatically land up next to you, you are expanding your interests, friendship group, activity opportunities and self-awareness. In fact, you're creating a wonderful life, and in wonderful lives, other wonderful things appear. Everyone wants to be with someone who is already happy and fulfilled. Make yourself that person regardless of whatever else is going on in your relationship or dating life.

Introducing yourself:

Don't think of this as an awkward thing to do, remember this person doesn't know you either, so whilst they're a stranger to you, you're also a stranger to them! Think of yourself as someone interesting they are about to meet and vice versa for them, and,

- Hi, my name is…
- I don't know anyone else here, do you?
- I like this a lot…
- This is funny/interesting/ unpleasant, isn't it?
- Can you help me with…?
- Do you know where the… is?
- That's a nice… you're wearing…
- Even, 'do you come here often?'

Any opener will do; it's just an ice-breaker saying to them 'it's ok to talk to me - in fact I'd like you to…'

An action plan:

One step at a time.

You don't need to go out there and create a full buzzing social life by the end of the first week, but if you set yourself an action plan, it has more chance of happening than if you say, 'oh well, I'll do that when I have time or the opportunity arises.' Usually we have to make time or create an opportunity for ourselves to do something we hadn't been doing before.

SMART goals will get you there – so make your plan of

Specific action: Join one new group or start one new activity or ritual each week.

Measure the results: Have a list and tick it off – have you joined the group / activity/completed the ritual this week?

Achievable for it: Which means don't set yourself impossible targets. Make it something you are comfortable doing and time, money and effort make it possible for you to actually do.

Relevant: Decide what they are going to be – perhaps as simple as having become involved in three new things by the end of the month, or having made three new acquaintances who you could call up to ask what's on, but which are relevant to improving your social life and being able to get out there and get the guy (or the girl).

Time-bound: Which means don't let yourself off the hook – set a time line for doing this and then follow it – just like Facebook!

So all of a sudden you're out there again and being sociable. Now is the tricky part of planning what you want in your future, setting boundaries for others' behaviour towards you, deciding on your life targets and aims, and taking steps to achieve them through what you're doing. Just getting out and about and kick-starting your social life is not necessarily enough. What if the type of guy or girl you're looking for doesn't frequent where you go? What happens when you start to date? How do you deal with other problems of relationships, kids, families, and their acceptance of your life? I'll give Pete a last word in this chapter before I go on my next date with him, because, surprisingly, he did ring after all!

'... every date starts off as being a one night stand, but if it's good enough to be a one night stand, then maybe it should stretch to 2 or more...'

Mmm, I already think we could start getting into some arguments here, so I'll obviously have to look at the whole sex issue later too. In the meantime, it's back to some more observation and strategy building when Pete and I meet next. This time I think I'm going to try to work out **what it means when...** because plainly when he said he would give me a call about going out again, and I thought he wouldn't, I was wrong...

Chapter 5: What it means when…

Now Pete said he would ask me out again and I didn't believe it so maybe I've just bumped straight into one of my own self-limiting beliefs? I'd been assuming I wasn't hot, but maybe I'm at least lukewarm?

One of the problems with men and women is that we speak from different angles - triangles even. It's like a man is an equilateral one and a woman is more sharp and questioning in her isosceles format. So as relationships are all about communicating with each other to build a bond, we obviously need to learn at least some of each other's language. Men use reasoning and logic; women tend to be more emotional, so that lends us towards being either pragmatic or emotional. That of course also influences the language we use and what we understand by it.

What is the definition of romantic? I looked up the definition in the dictionary - online of course because no-one needs to rustle through the musty pages of a dictionary any more. We're all in a quick-fix world, which maybe explains our inclination to internet date - the quick fix romance! It said 'sentimental, idealistic'. So are women sentimental and idealistic? Now we're heading into the realms of psychology, but it's an interesting idea to consider and why women might think that way because it gets us under their skin (or, I should say, my skin!) What do most

women set out to include in their lives if they have a life plan? Canvassing the women I knew, it was:
- Children.
- Nice home.
- Husband or partner.
- Happy life.
- Friends.
- Holidays.
- Looking nice.

...All in no particular order of preference.

What do men plan in their life spread-sheet? Asking them instead, it was:
- Career.
- Financial security.
- Achievement.
- Recognition.
- Quality car/motorbike/latest techy gadgets.
- Contentment.
- Mates.
- Steady or secure relationship and family.

Again they're all in no particular order, but we notice a very radical difference. Straightaway; the women's goals are all 'soft': nurturing, self-expanding in terms of the inner self. Yes they include more solid goals like a nice home and holidays, but these include a relative judgement with both of them - a 'nice' home and holidays by inference are suggestive of the feel-good factors of life, not the essentials.

Let's look at the guy's goals now. They are solid and factual: financial security, gadgets, and the feel-good factor is very much based on recognition and success - much more dominant and aggressive factors. Well, obviously men and women are a bit different aren't they? Men are the hunter-gatherers and women are the nurturers. But that brings us back to the root of the problem between us; we approach things differently. Notice there are some things both men and women want though, the home, the steady base, the relationship, the friends/mates - but with the male/female spin on them, depending on whether it's a man or a woman talking about them. So maybe we actually want exactly the same things, and if we could just talk the same language to each other we both might get them. Could the problem be easily solved by us each learning each other's lingo? Let's have a look at the vocabulary...

Whatever a guy's motivation for using his own cryptic communication; avoiding a conflict, fishing for clues before he makes himself vulnerable, or trying to avoid hurting your feelings, the sooner girls understand what guy code is really saying, and guys decipher girl language, the less confusion and heartache there will be in our relationships. This list is by no means exhaustive, and really it's just representative because the guy or girl you meet will also put their own gloss on it with their own specific language style and also based on their past experiences. What it does do is make you think about what the pragmatic man is really meaning, and the emotional girl is getting at, *before* you jump in with both feet and end up knee deep in muddy water!

Man speak v woman speak – a dictionary…

Man speak phrase	What he means	What she means	The bone of contention…
"We should do something sometime".	"I want to ask you out, but I don't want to feel rejected if you say no."	"He's going to ask me out, I'll sit back and wait."	Girls – give the guy a thumbs up won't you?
"Do you think we can still be friends?"	"I'm not really attracted to you, but I think you're cool and would like to hang out as buddies."	"He's rejecting me."	He's not rejecting you, or vice versa if a girl is saying this to a guy. Just take the message at face value – if someone thinks you're cool, cool is great any way it comes – accept it gracefully!
"Maybe we should take a break and see other people."	"There's someone else I'm interested in and I want to feel free to test the waters."	"He's a commitment-a-phobe."	Guy's be honest as well as tactful, and girls – well, show him what he's missing with the pleasure pain principle – explained later on in the book.
"It would	"I'm not	"He's scared of	Sometimes-

be great to date you, but I don't want to ruin our friendship"	interested in sleeping with you, but I think you're a great person and I don't want to hurt your feelings."	dating me/ a commitment-a-phobe."	despite claims to the contrary – you can just **like** someone but not romantically or physically – so go with it; friends are always great!
"That's an *interesting* outfit."	"Whatever that is you're wearing, you should go and change immediately."	"He thinks I'm unusual/stylish."	Guys, risk the wrath – if she looks like an idiot, say so. When a girls says 'does my bum look big in this?' she does actually want to know if she looks ok or not. Be honest (diplomatically, but not cryptically).
"Come hang out at…… I'll be hanging out with my friends."	"Sure we can hang out, but I want to make sure you don't think of this as a date."	"I'm being invited on a date in a round-about way."	Hanging out with friends is not a date, unless you're already dating and you're going as a **couple.**

"Let's not jump into anything just yet and see how things go."	"I'm interested in you, but I still want to see other people right now."	"He's frightened of commitment. I just need to convince him we're good together long term."	Girls if he's not exclusive with you, spend your time on him in direct proportion to his commitment to you and the priority he is giving you in his life. Guys- learn that this is what happens if you want to test the waters elsewhere too
"Oh, her? She's just an old friend."	"We have probably either had sex or dated at some point but it's not relevant to you and therefore none of your business."	"She's an old flame and she's a threat."	If he's with you, then accept that for face value. His behaviour around the other girl will tell you how much of an old flame or an old friend she currently is, and then act accordingly yourself.
"It's not you, it's	"This relationship is	"Poor guy, he needs me to	If he says it's him - it is him -

me."	not working for me, and if I take the blame then I don't have to hurt your feelings by listing the reasons why I'm not interested in you anymore."	help him with whatever issue he has in committing to me."	or rather **he** doesn't have the right feelings for you. Let him go, you warrant someone having all the right feelings for you.
I'll get to it in a minute"	"I'll get to it when I feel like it, not when you think I should."	"He needs nagging to remind him what I've already asked him to do…"	If you nag, he'll lag even more. Find a way to make him want to do whatever it is you want him to – see behaviour modelling later on.
"Guys are always checking you out, I must be a lucky guy."	"I'm feeling self-conscious from all the attention you are getting and need reassurance that you are happy with me and not	"He's proud of me."	Reassure the poor guy (and secretly enjoy how hot you obviously are!)

	interested in any of these guys who are flirting with you."		
"You and that guy seem like good friends."	"Did you guys ever date?"	"He's suspicious of me and…"	Tell him the basics of what he needs to know, if he needs to know any history you have with the guy, reassure him that he is the one you are interested in now.
"We are planning our divorce, but due to financial reasons we are still living together."	"I'm too afraid to leave her – I want to be with both of you for as long as I can stretch it."	"Complicated but single."	If he's living with a woman – any woman, it's not what it seems and you are probably just the jam on the bread. You're not a bit of confectionary so scrape yourself off the bread and find someone for

			whom you are bread, butter and jam.
"I'll call you…"	"If I remember or am still interested in a little while's time, I WILL call you (but not if I'm not!)."	"I'm expecting you to call me tomorrow – or maybe even later on today…"	Men are the do-ers, let them do. Women are the responders, so let it happen. Don't chase if they don't call you. After all they have said they will, and if they don't its because they're not that interested after all…
"Maybe we could do this again…"	"I would like to date you but I'm playing it cautious as I don't know how keen you are?"	"I'm expecting to do this again straightaway and will be waiting (impatiently) to hear from you about the next date…"	Women are home-makers, nurturers and deal in practicalities, which means the shopping gets done, the dentist appointments get made, the dress is chosen well beforehand for the next date. Men slip through life

			responding as it happens. Don't try to be his secretary as well as his date!
"I'm tactile and romantic…"	"I hope that if we click, it will lead to sex on the first – or second – date…"	"I expect you to hold my hand, say romantic things to me and we'll have a long lingering kiss- Mills and Boon style – to presage the start of a wonderful relationship…"	Pragmatic man: romantic woman.
"Let's see how it goes…"	"I'm not making any commitments to being exclusive with you until I'm sure I want to and that means I will be dating other women too…"	"This man is a player…"	Seeing how it goes actually isn't playing, it is merely demonstrating that one or more of the people involved isn't sure yet and wants to leave their options open. For a choice to be a real choice, the chooser has to make the

			choice and stick to it voluntarily. Let that happen without pre-judging and maybe you will be pleasantly surprised by the choice made. However, equally, only give him the proportionate time back that he is giving you as he sees 'how it goes', and see how it goes for you too...
"Really?"	"I'm not listening."	"He wants to know more so I'll tell him..."	Pay attention – she'll catch you out...
"We've had this argument before."	"I remember not listening then too."	"So why didn't you pay attention then?"	Time to start paying attention to each other – seriously!

"OK then."	"You're wrong, but I am withdrawing from the fight in an attitude of wounded martyrdom."	"I've won…"	Road block ahead.
"What's wrong?"	"What meaningless self-inflicted psycho trauma are you going through now?"	"Nothing… (see below)."	Oops – trouble ahead…

The antonym to romantic ('opposite' before we all go rushing back to Google and check out the word) is 'pragmatic, realistic' – and here we have it - women v men. So if we perceive our lives with that spin on them, then obviously we are going to approach the facets of our lives with the same inclinations, and if we are to bridge the gap between us we need to learn how to figure out each other's take on it all and apply it to ours – hey presto: understanding!

So how is it (romantic) women present themselves to (pragmatic) men? Hmm, time to look at this in more detail… Women speak - what does it mean?

Woman speak phrase	What she means	What he means	The bone of contention...
"Are you seeing anyone right now?"	"I might like to submit an application for the position of your girlfriend."	"She's keen – I'm in!"	She wants to make sure she is not wasting her precious flirting energy on a man who is already spoken for. **What you should do:** Answer honestly, and then hit her for her phone number.
"I don't want to ruin our friendship."	"I am not attracted to you, or I don't feel enough chemistry to date you -- but I do like you as friend."	"She's playing hard to get".	She probably does want to remain friends, but doesn't want to hurt your feelings by admitting that she doesn't feel the same attraction for you. **What you should do:** Don't take it personally;

			she just doesn't feel the same chemistry as you do. Take the hint and work on being friends with her, if that's what you want.
"I'm just so busy with work right now."	"I am not interested in fitting you into my schedule."	"Poor girl, I'll be encouraging".	She wants to let you down easy. Instead of being blunt, she is hoping you'll just get the picture. **What you should do:** When a woman likes a man, she will always find time for him – no matter what her schedule is like. So don't kid yourself into thinking that the situation

			might change. Instead, move on right away.
"Fine."	"It's not fine actually."	"That's ok then…"	This is the word women use to end an argument when they are right and you need to shut up.
"Nothing."	"Actually it's a lot; I'm just not saying any of it at the moment!"	"That's ok then…"	This is the calm before the storm. This means something, not 'nothing', and you should be on your toes. Arguments that begin with nothing usually end in fine.
"Go right ahead."	"Don't you dare…"	"I can then, can I…"	This is a dare, not permission… Don't Do It!

"That's OK."	"That's very not ok."	"That's ok."	This is one of the most dangerous statements a women can make to a man. 'That's OK' means she wants him to think long and hard before deciding as she's thinking long and hard how and when he will pay for the mistake.
"Thanks."	"I'm not thanking you, I'm being sarcastic."	"Wow!"	A woman is thanking you; do not question, or faint. Just say 'you're welcome.' (I want to add in a clause here – This is true, unless she says 'Thanks a lot' – that is pure sarcasm and she is not

				thanking you at all. Do not say 'you're welcome'... that will bring on a 'whatever').
"Whatever."	"You've pushed me to far now…"	"Ok we'll leave it there, then…"	Is a women's way of saying: ---- you!
"Don't worry about it, I've got it."	"I've asked you to do it several times, but now I'm doing it myself and I'm not happy…"	'What's wrong?'	When the man asks 'What's wrong?' the woman's response will be 'nothing'…
"Really?"	"Tell me more."	"I'm not listening."	Road block ahead!
"We've had this argument before."	"And you didn't make any sense then."	"I remember not listening then too."	Road block ahead!
"OK then."	"Prove it!"	"You're wrong, but I am withdrawing from the fight	Road block ahead!

			in an attitude of wounded martyrdom."	

Now where shall I go from here? Back to Pete I think and listen to what he was saying to me on our second date and see if I can decipher the true meanings, and also if we can actually mould our potential partner's behaviour by the language we use.

This time we went out for a meal. I wondered if he was listening as carefully to what I was saying as he was – let's see - the words are in black, the man/woman speak is in script - where was our conversation leading?

'You look very nice?'

'Thank you.'

'What would you like?' *(So far so good, he'd complimented me and was attentive).*

'A dry white wine please.' I smiled encouragingly at him.

'So, Debbie, have you been doing anything interesting today?'

'Yes, actually I've been doing something fascinating for me...' and I started to tell him about my strategy project, until I realised from his slightly glazed expression over my left shoulder that he was focussing elsewhere already, so I paused. He obviously had enough attention on me still to belatedly realise I'd stopped talking and added his own contribution to what had been my soliloquy:

"Really?" (*I'm not listening*, *but then I already knew that, and now I also could see that actually he was distracted by another blonde*)

'Yes, so I thought I would wear my stockings and suspenders tonight just for the occasion.'

'What? (**Ah now he was listening…**)

'At the party I'm going to next week. My costume…'

'Oh, I see. What party is that?'

'Never mind.' (**Why am I bothering?**) I changed tack: 'I was wondering what you thought about that article in the paper yesterday?'

'Which one was that?' (*The blonde floated past and left a whiff of expensive perfume with us. His eyes strayed off in her direction as he replied.*)

'The one on men and women's ability to focus; when distracted by the opposite sex.' I replied sarcastically. (*Well, who wouldn't be starting to feel a little rankled by his straying attention now?*)

He must have noticed the sharp edge to my tone and brought his attention firmly back to me. 'Sorry, you were saying?'

"Don't worry about it' (*I've asked you several questions several times, without your attention being on me and now I'm not happy…*)

'Is everything ok? You seem a little flustered.'

'No, nothing's wrong.' (*Actually there's a lot wrong; I'm just not saying any of it at the moment!*)

'Oh, that's ok, then…*(pause)* Actually, would you mind, just a moment; it's just that – well, that blonde I told you about is over there and I'd just like to… Well, I'll be right back…' He did at least have the decency to wait for me to give him leave with my,

'go right ahead' (*in other words, 'don't you dare'*), but when he came back all smiles and said to me, 'so, what were we talking about.' What else could I say but 'nothing' (*This is the calm before the storm. This means something, and you should be on your toes.*)

Of course it didn't progress to an argument; I didn't know him well enough to, but to his suggestion at the end of an evening punctuated by him smiling devilishly at the perfumed blonde:

'Maybe we could do this again, and see how it goes…' (*Two messages here! He is playing it cautious… 1. If I remember or am still interested in a little while's time, I WILL call you – but not if I'm not! And 2. I'm not making any commitments to being exclusive with you until I'm sure I want to and that means I will be dating other women too…*) No doubt the hot blonde if at all possible. My reply could only be one thing:

'Whatever.'

Now obviously I came home very unhappy with the whole evening. This man had asked me out, not paid attention to me and actually wandered off to chat up some other woman during the course of the evening too. Not only was it demeaning to me, it was downright insulting too. What had I done wrong? I sat down and replayed the whole evening like it was a DVD in reverse, and then added in the parts of the strategy that I'd established so far. Ah now I stated to see where I'd gone wrong.

- First I'd allowed him to walk completely over the boundary of my principles and standards, which said if you're on a date with Debbie you pay her the appropriate full attention to demonstrate respect for her – after all you asked her out so why wouldn't you want to pay attention to her?
- Secondly I'd not picked up on the man speak language and tackled it immediately – the 'really?' and all the conversation (or lack of it) which followed afterwards which so amply demonstrated to me that he wasn't listening and therefore wasn't demonstrating any respect for me.
- Thirdly I'd effectively sanctioned his bad behaviour in going off to chat up another women by allowing him to go and then accepting him back when he'd done so. It was like I'd actually rewarded his bad behaviour so he assumed I didn't mind. Of course now, he would think it alright to continue in that behaviour and wonder what the matter was if I objected later on. I could almost hear him saying, 'but you said it was ok?'

- Finally, he had no idea from my behaviour what my principles or standards were because I hadn't demonstrated them in any way. In fact I'd demonstrated the reverse to what I felt whilst silently fuming away at him.

I decide to rephrase the whole conversation and re-model the whole behaviour set in my mind and see how different the outcome would have been. Then I tried it out the next time his eyes strayed – the outcome was very different and you can read it all in the next chapter…

Chapter 6: 'Mirror, mirror on the wall…' What attraction is all about.

It's the little things that make that certain spark happen - the very little things; neurons in fact. Here's a bit of science-speak for you: inside the brain are some very specific nerve cells called 'mirror neurons'. They allow us to relate specifically to other humans in a particular way. How can you explain the irresistible urge to yawn when you see someone else yawn? Mirror neurons. They are a kind of special circuitry in our brains that explain the phenomena, as well as many other circumstances where people's brains actually become wired to one another.

Researchers from the University of Parma in Italy stumbled upon these amazing neurons when they were studying planning movements in monkeys. They were testing a particular neuron that made a specific sound whenever a monkey would grab for a peanut and observed something one day that made them sit up with surprise. While a monkey was sitting idly, one of the researchers came in and just picked up a peanut. The monkey's cell fired even though it had not moved. He merely watched the human grasp the peanut and the neuron fired. The same neuron fired both when the monkey observed something and when it was doing something. *(3.)*

Further study established that this neuron seemed to mirror the movement it sees. Some researchers subsequently called them the 'monkey see, monkey do' neurons, but the Italian scientists labelled them the much more professionally sounding *'mirror neurons'*. Subsequent studies have shown that mirror neurons are also found in the human brain *(4.)*, so seeing someone do something is the same as doing it yourself.

Imagine how many times you guys have seen a character in a film kicked in the un-mentionables and responded with a wince and an 'ouch'. These neurons enable us to relate to the experience of others as well as to empathise and learn from them. These clever little neurons relate us to other people's actions as well as to their feelings, so they represent part of the way the brain's translates and interprets the way we relate to the world around us - and of course the people in it.

So, enough of blinding us all with scientific genius; what does this all mean in real terms? Well the mirror neuron enables us to metaphorically 'live' in other people's minds and bodies. Mirror neurons help us to adopt others perceptions as well as to connect us emotionally. Perhaps this suggests that deep down - down to the very basic structure of our cells, we are built to be together. There is something very reassuring about that, but also powerfully useful for all of us looking for the right guy or the right girl…

I started off by realising that in order to narrow down the field and find the right guy (or right girl) I needed to establish specifically what I liked best, what I valued, who I was. Well of course that set me off in the right direction and gave the Man-nav (or Sat-girl for you guys) a chance to navigate in the best direction, but once you get to the right destination, what next? How do you ensure that they respond to YOU, become attracted to YOU? Ah, that's where the mirror neurons jump in to help.

Mirror neurons encourage the other person to mirror your behaviour and you to mirror theirs. Now there are two benefits to this:

- Flattery is a wonderful thing for encouraging someone to like you - they say copying is the most sincere form of flattery, don't they? So when you mirror your potential date target, and they mirror you back, you are both indulging in an awful lot of reciprocal flattery.
- And then, the clever girl or the smart guy also knows that if they subtly adapt what they're doing, the other person will respond with a subtle change to their behaviour too - those little mirror neurons won't take no for an answer.

Hey presto! All of a sudden you have the makings of behaviour manipulation - or 'modelling' at your fingertips. All I needed to know now were the kinds of things that encouraged initial attraction and response, so I thought I'd study Pete's reactions a bit more and find out what he was attracted to.

I watched him closely on our next 'date' - because there was one. This was becoming more surprising all the time. We again sat politely at the bar for the pre-dinner drink, but as I walked in,

I smiled straight into the eyes of another man and he turned round to look at me more fully. Then I winked at the bar man as he put an extra cherry in my cocktail and lastly I sat with my back to the bar and facing out into the room - looking at and being seen by everyone; not with my back to the room as I had before. I straightened my dress as I did so, deciding I might have to curtail the dinners out - I was starting to put on weight. Pete smiled at me and I smiled sweetly back, tipping my head down a bit. I'd been reading a book on the 50 basic flirting signs just before he picked me up so I thought I try some of them out and see which worked best. I looked at him through my lashes -– this apparently was called the 'peek-a-boo' - or was it the 'Diana'? I couldn't remember, but I carried on with it and continued smiling too. He edged a fraction closer - well that obviously went down well. I just hoped those little mirror neurons wouldn't pick up on the game and make him mirror it as that would make me laugh. He didn't, but he did start the conversation by saying I looked very pretty. What did I say in reply? A polite thank-you, or something more playful? I decided playful was probably the order of the day - after all, I was trying to flirt wasn't it?

'Thanks, Mr Charmer - shall I tell you how sexy you look too, or have you already been told that?' I winked, and touched him lightly on the inside of his forearm as it rested on the bar, hand curled round his pint. The reaction was electric. He openly preened himself, and then lightly stroked my arm with the back of his fore finger and paid me another compliment back.

'Not as hot as you look tonight - actually I didn't want to be too forward, but you really do look great.' Well that was much better than 'you look pretty tonight', wasn't it? I'd better keep this going. I tested out one of the flirting actions next. My shoe slipped gently off the heel of my foot and swung tantalisingly as I chatted. Pete answered my small talk about what he'd been doing today but I noticed his eyes slide down to my feet - no *my foot* - and stay there a moment, watching the dangling red stiletto, then they slid back up my leg and lingered mid crutch level until they eventually made their way back to my face. He realised I was watching him when his eyes met mine and blushed. How amazing, I'd never seen a man blush like that before - but it did bear out two things I'd read:

> 1. Men cannot be subtle when they're sizing you up physically, so ladies just live with it - at least they ARE sizing you up, a sure sign of interest.

> 2. The swinging stiletto worked.

'Nice shoes,' was all he said. I had to stifle my explosion of laughter very quickly. I hid it by crossing and re-crossing my legs: another flirting signal. Pete obliged by watching my legs again and then adding a bit of his own flirting language back - the 'visual undress'. After he'd given me a complete all-over sweep and decided what colour underwear I had on under the dress, I took myself off to the ladies to get my clothes back on and check my make-up, employing the 'film-star wiggle' walk as I went. Whew - sexual tension, or what?

Well, flirting obviously creates an initial attraction - what was it about flirting that worked so well, I wondered? I spent slightly longer in the ladies than I should have wondering about that, retouching my make-up and straightening my dress as I did so. Thinking about what I'd done/was doing, I decided it was this:

- Living in the moment: Not having an expectation to live up to or a target to achieve, just doing whatever I was doing and responding to how it worked out. In other words, I didn't expect Pete to respond, I didn't worry any longer if Pete responded or not, and if he did, I just reacted however it seemed right at the time - I was spontaneous.
- Being pro-active: I smiled, I teased, I winked, I looked and I got looked back at. Suddenly I wasn't a mousy miss in tow behind Pete. I was a sexy siren, marching in front of him. I'd gone up several notches in the desirable ratings because of it.
- Being confident: I imagined I oozed it now, with the proactive body language, the openly looking stance. It is exciting to be with someone confident in themselves - it had been part of the attraction to Pete in the first place, his self-confidence.
- Being open: I was no longer the shy retiring me that Pete had first met. Having growing confidence in myself as I started to follow through my plan had also made me more open about what I thought, what I wanted, what I would and wouldn't accept. In turn, that made me more like that 'high value' person I'd identified was the key

to it all when I'd first started wondering what it was that would attract Pete. I was starting to openly declare my 'requirements' with the way I was behaving. I didn't actually have to put them into words.

- <u>Being tactile</u>: Touch - one of the most explosive of senses. We can't help but touch things, to feel what they are like. Touch between humans is the thing that creates the physical bond. Touch someone and you create a little bit of ownership between them and you: you've broken the ice, jumped the barrier; made it OK for them to touch you back - Pete certainly thought so!
- <u>Creating sexual tension</u> : Oh yes, I'd certainly done that, through the swinging stiletto, the wink, the crossing legs and the film star wiggle. Such simple little things to do...

So if flirting was so easy to do, maybe it was time to catalogue all those flirtatious little opportunities that helped add to the confident daters approach. I decided to try to work through all the girl flirts I could think of that evening and observe the responding ones from Pete. It was a long evening! I didn't quite make the 50, but there were enough of the biggies to be going on with, I reckoned.

From the top: flirting with your eyes

1. The lingering look - and don't look away. How will they know you find them attractive if you look away as soon as they look at you? Take a deep breath and stay focussed - on them!

2. The flirt triangle. Look from eyes to mouth and then back to their eyes again. Why? It's suggesting that you would like them to kiss you; that's why you're looking at their mouth, right? (Not because they've got a crumb stuck to the corner of it).

3. Looking away and back. Ok, this is one to do if you lose your nerve on the long lingering look - look back again. Go on, you CAN do it, and they'll know you're interested if you do. What happens when you know someone is interested in you? You automatically look back at them - those damn mirror neurons again!

4. The peek-a-boo look. OK, I've decided that this one is a version of the Diana look, but shorter and cheekier. You look up at them through your eyelashes, then look away, and then look back again. What is it saying? I'm shy but I like you so much I can't resist another look - come and get me...

5. The mouth stare. Just keep looking (and still ignore that irritating little crumb). It says 'mmmm, kiss me...' (But get rid of the crumb first please).

Under the eyes and onto flirting with your mouth:

6. Eating anything on your date? Ideal: suck it sensuously - I don't need to spell out what that suggests, do I?

7. Lick your lips - but not too obviously, and NOT like the kid licking his lips as he laboriously concentrates on doing his school homework. That's not sensuous at all.

8. Most dates entail having a drink at some stage, so you have more props - a glass preferably as it's not so sexy with a cup. (Looks like you've lost your way to the vicar's tea party with a cuppa!) Lick it - you know what that means - back to number 6 in fact, but with a different prop.

9. This generally only works for a woman, (but I suppose life is full of new experiences) but leaving your lipstick stain on a glass can be sexy. It gives the guy the opportunity to see your lips twice over - real and imprinted, and let his imagination run riot. On the other hand, he might be thinking, 'that would be a pain to have to wash off', so test the water carefully first.

Still at the top: flirting with your hair

10. If you've got it, flaunt it - long hair flicks back cheekily and sexily - and most men secretly fantasise about the woman with the long legs and the long hair to go with it, it's a fantasy stereotype.

11. Expose yourself just a little bit. Some areas of the body are particularly sensuous, and carry the connotation of desire and seduction with them. One of them is the neck - 'he kissed the nape of her neck and her body thrilled to his touch as his lips moved softly down onto her shoulder and...' Other ones are the inside of the wrist, the inside of the upper arm, and if you are kissing, running your fingers up through their hair from the nape of their neck is... enough said!

12. Want a bit of 'come hither'? Look back over the shoulder at them. It says, 'I'm going, and look what you're missing out on - you'd better run after me quick.'

Moving down a bit: flirting with your voice

13. Voices are sexier the lower the tone of them. No, I don't mean lower the tone, I mean lower the tone; deeper, huskier, sexier. Would you fancy a woman who sounded like Minnie Mouse, or a man who had been inhaling helium?

14. Now you *can* lower the tone though, with a bit of innuendo - it creates that sexual tension, but not too low. Remember you're still high value but with a sexy twist on it.

Lower still: let your fingers do the talking

15. Play with objects - the wine glass stem, the napkin - but do it sensuously, like you would play with them...

16. Flash the stash again - one of those teasingly seductive areas of bare flesh, the inner under arm - either the top of the arm, or the inner wrist - see 11 again.

17. Touch yourself if you can't touch them (although of course you can - see 18 below). It means this is where you could touch me too...

18. Touch THEM-— but be careful where as some places are good and some are taboo. Good places: the inner arm, the inside of the wrist, the chest (on a man) - there's nothing sexier than a woman lightly stroking a man's chest - the shoulder, the knee, but careful here - not too high up the thigh. We're talking a different language if you get any higher than just above the knee.

19. Groom yourself. Stroke your hair back into place, smooth your dress - it's all an invitation to the other person to do the same to you.

Down to the legs: all the way down!

20. Cross and uncross those legs, ladies - he just can't help but look.

21. Now this is a really tricky one as done skilfully, it can be enormously tempting. Done badly and you look like a bad cross between Dame Edna Everage and Lily Savage. With legs uncrossed, let your knees slip slightly apart so there is just the slightest suggestion that there are no barriers here. Too far apart and you'll be displaying your thong to all and sundry - woe betide you if it's crotchless!

23. If you're sitting close enough together. Let your knee brush his, just lightly; oh-oh! Electric reaction there!

24. The shoe dangle - works best with high heels or stilettos, and doesn't work at all if your shoes have ankle straps. Guys, don't even bother reading this one.

And posture: using the space

25. Lean in and invade their space, not for too long though as that's just awkward, but it suggests this is how close WE could be...

26. The boob thrust: another if you've got it, flaunt it more. You don't need boundless boobs to make this work, even a little bit of cleavage works nicely, as you show'em what you've got. Make sure you've got plenty of space round you so you don't knock a glass over and ruin the show, then put both hands back behind your head as if you were stretching and arch your back just slightly. Oh, what a wonderful view; and you've just shared it. Thank you ma'am! Guys, sadly, this one isn't for you either, but

you can enjoy being on the receiving end and knowing exactly what your date is saying to you…

27. Standing, you can still make an impression with your posture. Hand on hip, slightly teapot-style; just don't complete it by making a spout with the other arm, please. It says I'm a sassy lady, and throws out just a hint of a challenge without being intimidating. Guys can do this too - it says 'here I am ladies', but careful not to look camp.

28. The film-star wiggle, which works best as you walk away. Make sure they have a clear view - you're not going to risk pulling a muscle if they're not getting a good view of the full works, and do make sure you haven't got your skirt tucked into your knickers, Bridget Jones-style. There are film stars, and there are *film stars*…

These were mainly what the ladies do, but guys flirt too. Make the most of knowing what both sexes do so you can decipher the body lingo.

Here are the guys' grabbers:

29. First of all there's 'the eye you up' - a look all the way up and down - completely open; there's no mistaking the interest.

30. Then there may be the slow eyebrow raise, the one that's says 'oh, hello…'

31. Guys are no good at hiding their interest or being subtle about it like women are. That's not a criticism, it's just the way women and men behave differently. In fact the guys make it so much easier for the girls to read the signs than the girls do for the guys. If a guy is interested in a girl, he will make no bones about it. He won't slyly eye you and look away when you look, he'll turn right around and LOOK.

32. Guys might undress you with their look - Pete did. Good job I had my best matching underwear on.

33. Guys may well peacock it. Remember how the male peacock creates that wonderful display of tail feathers to the female when they're trying to attract them as a mate? Well, why shouldn't the guys show off their pecs, their sexy chest, their six pack (as long as it's not cans)? Girls swing their stiletto, cross and uncross their legs, flick their hair and lick their lips: it's all the same thing.

34. Self-preening or grooming is much the same thing as 33. Except, the guy is trying to focus the girl on the articular part of himself he wants to show off by his body language.

35. Bragging or boasting is also much the same thing, but verbal.

36. And then a guy can get touch-feely as well: he can lean in and invade the girls' space too.

37. A favourite touchy-feely, because it comes across as manly and protective is to lightly brush the woman's cheek. Ooh, women love a man with a sensitive side.

38. And yes, he can tease a girl too to make her react; but make sure the reaction is a playful one.

Isn't it interesting to note the basic difference between men and women when flirting? Women are more subtle and they have many more flirting signals than men - 28 that I thought of, to men's 10. It means that it's much more obvious to a woman when a man is flirting with her because his signals are also much more direct, whereas women's are subtle, and sometimes masked by other behaviour. To the straight-thinking, objective guy, it's a potential mine-field he might get blown out of at any time. What is the best policy here then, to avoid the guy missing the signal and the girl missing the guy? Make it as obvious as you can, so those days of being too shy to LOOK have to go. Pro-active is really the watchword here: pro-active and fearless, the new kind of dating woman. Guys, you have been warned!

Now of course we can't always get (exactly) what we want - wait didn't someone sing a song about that? But we can get close to what we want and add a helping hand for the rest. Let's go back to establishing our principles and values and consider the guy who hasn't got a big actively involved family around him. Maybe one or both of his parents are dead and he had no brothers and sisters. It's hard to be a family man without a family, but he may have a strong sense of family values nevertheless, just not know how to put them into action. Cue the smart girl and her little mirror neurons and *modelling* the kind behaviour patterns you want. How? Well I tried it out on Pete, in a different kind of scenario but the principle was the same - go back to see how effective it was.

Mine and Pete's jealousy scene - similar to the last chapter but this time Pete gets modelled!

Stage direction: Pete looks at the hot blonde - the new script is underlined…

'You look very nice?'

'Thank you.'

'What would you like?' **(*So far so good, he'd complimented me and was attentive*)**

'A dry white wine please.' I smiled encouragingly at him.

'So, Debbie, have you been doing anything interesting today?'

'Yes, actually I've been doing something fascinating for me, <u>**what do you think it was?**</u>' (*There's the challenge to keep his attention focused on me.*)

'<u>I don't know - tell me?</u>' (*His expression is curious and attentive*). So I started to tell him about my strategy project, until I realised from his slightly glazed expression over my left shoulder that he was focussing elsewhere already, so I paused.

'<u>Have you seen someone you know?</u>'

'Oh, just a friend.' (A woman he'd dated, or wanted to).

'Oh, who is that?'

'Oh, not important.'

He returned his attention to me and I carried on.

'Shall I tell you some more about what I've been doing or would you like to tell me what you've been up to as well, Mr Wandering Eyes ?' (Teasing and playful).

'Wandering eyes? I'm not, I'm all ears!'

'Well, I'll tell you some more if you'd like?'

'Fire away, Miss Telling Me Off!'

I continued with my soliloquy but it wasn't long before the blonde I knew he'd been distracted by caught his eye again.

'Really?' (The blonde floated past and left a whiff of expensive perfume with us. His eyes strayed off in her direction as he replied).

'Actually, would you mind, just a moment; it's just that - well, that blonde I told you about is over there and I'd just like to...well - I'll be right back...'

'Go right ahead' (in other words, 'don't you dare') but when he came back all smiles and said to me,

'so, what were we talking about?' I replied.

'We were talking about what I'd been doing today but it's such a turn-off when a guy isn't listening to what you say.' I smiled at him and sipped my drink. He reddened.

'I'm sorry...'

'Well, if you want to ask me out then I would expect you to want to spend your time with me, not chatting up some other woman in front of me. I respect you more than to do that to you, and to be honest, it makes me really not interested in a guy if he's not polite to the lady he's with.'

Now Pete is squirming. 'Gosh, I'm really sorry. That was rude, you're right.'

'Well I'll let you off this once, but now you owe me, don't you?' and I looked at him archly over my drink and winked cheekily.

'What the lady wants, the lady gets…' He looked so relieved I wasn't going to ear-bash him anymore. The point was made and taken. I almost laughed, but I kept my calm demeanour and changed the subject to a funny story I'd heard on the radio that morning.

To his suggestion at the end of an evening **significantly avoiding looking at the** perfumed blonde:

'Maybe we could do this again? *(I would like to date you but I'm playing it cautious as I don't know how keen you are?)* My reply could only be,

'**Maybe, give me a call and I'll see if I'm free.**' *(But only if you try hard, because I'm a high value woman, you see…).*

Now that was a far more satisfactory ending and it brought into play all my principles, standards, man and woman-speak and re-modelled his behaviour to the way I wanted it by praising and rewarding what I liked and telling him that his bad behaviour would be a turn off. Not- not a telling off, telling him it was a turn-off. No man wants to be a turn-off. Another part of the strategy was in place, and proof that the type of language used does make a difference. Tell him it turns you off, he'll never do it again. Tell him it turns you on and he'll offer to do it till the cows come home, but significantly, say it all in a calm collected manner. It can't then be a 'what's wrong?' (*What meaningless self-inflicted psycho trauma are you going through now?*), it can only be a logical statement of requirements that pragmatic man understands and respects. Now we're motoring!

    Guys you can do this with the girls too, of course. If she eyes up another guy, you can subtly imply that any girl who checks out the other guys when she's with him isn't very classy. No girl worth dating wants to regarded as, 'not classy'- see what I mean? Choose the language carefully and model the behaviour you want in what you imply you regard as valuable and desirable, and the mirror neurons pick up on it and automatically programme the recipient to respond in the right way. Those little things are your best friend when establishing attraction and behaviour requirements. Pay attention to them when you go on your next date and see how much better the response is!

Chapter 7 Lets give the shy guys and the shrinking violets some super tips:

Going back to this idea that men and women come at relationships and dating from two different directions, it probably helps if you have at least a fixing point for where the start is. Now the last thing I would call Pete was shy. Some of his stories made me cringe in fact. For instance, his story about the 'Telecoms date', and how they 'connected on every route across the world', as he crudely put it. She was an American, with a high-powered job in the communication industry that took her across the world regularly. When in town, she'd been looking for a quick date for the night; 'all-inclusive', as it were. Pete had obliged and earned himself extra fringe benefits with free international travel as her 'companion' whenever it suited. He even expected to join the mile high club at some point along the route. Obviously Pete wasn't shy - and nor was she, but what about the many guys and girls that are? All very well to urge them and me to be proactive, but being proactive is daunting to say the least. Even if we do understand what the reactions mean and what to do next to capitalise on them to achieve that gold-dust *right date*, it's still scary.

    I wondered how to tackle that problem for a long time before I pieced together the next bit of the strategy, because a shrinking violet was in truth probably the right description for me, despite my preponderance for 6500 feet jumps. Maybe the shy guy was the nice right guy I would like to meet, but would he be too shy to approach me? Most likely I would have to do the approaching myself and then model him away from his shyness to get any further. I decided to tackle confidence issues first because if you aren't confident enough to make an approach, you're never going to get any further than looking, are you?

Confidence boosting!

A big part of being confident is projecting that image to the world.

Guys: Are you projecting a shy Mommy's boy to the world, or do you approach life like a MAN? Do you look like someone who's got balls and would defend himself in a fight if he had to, or do you look like you'd offer to hold the other guys coat? Do you appear to live on the adventurous side of life or spend your evening on with your play station, killing zombies and aliens? In other words, do you look like you'd be interesting to know?

Girls: Do you look like the office girl who never goes out, dresses in last years' fashions, wears flatties because they're more comfortable than heels, never tries out a new sport or club because she's not sure if she'd make a fool of herself?

In other words, guy or girl:

- Do you do things that are exciting or new?
- Do you take risks sometimes?
- Do you smile and talk to strangers, simply because you don't know them - yet?
- Do you have a passion or a belief you're prepared to stand up and speak out for?
- Do you think that, whatever your faults, you're actually an OK person to meet?

OR

- Do you just live the same routine, day in and day out?

Being confident is partly to do with the way you see yourself, and partly the way you project yourself and therefore how others respond to you - reinforcing the way you see yourself. If every day is just a repeat of the day before, and you always have everything planned in advance, taking the cautious approach, unfortunately you will remain one of the guys or girls who get put automatically in the 'friend zone', and never get out of it: a *safe* guy or a *nice* girl, but not one anyone looks to date. The safe guys and the nice girls are always wondering how to get out of the 'friend zone' because they re-affirm their place in it continuously by the way they continue to behave. So, it's time to break the mould and project yourself as something other than *safe* or *nice*. It's time to be bit extraordinary - because we all are; we just have to find the celebrity inside us that everyone wants to meet, and be brave enough to put them out there in the spotlight.

How do you become that extraordinary person who projects confidence so well, that they suddenly ARE confident, and finding all kinds of dates as a result? Begin by assessing yourself and the image you're projecting to the world, and start to transform it by improving the parts of it that can be changed without taking you out of your comfort zone.

10 Things you can do to build social confidence:

1. Turn self-consciousness into self-awareness , so instead of saying I can't do this because... Tell yourself 'I feel awkward doing this because, so I'm going to (insert your idea)... instead', and find a solution that enables you to do whatever it is that is difficult for you. For example, if you feel awkward going somewhere new where you know no-one, co-opt a friend for the first occasions you go somewhere new until you've met and got to know a few people. The next time, you can free-fall because you now know people to talk to straight away. This is finding ways to turn anxiety into positive action-taking instead.
2. Find your strengths: Write at least 5 of them down daily, and remind yourself of them whenever you are feeling unsure or nervous. By the end of a week you'll have 35 or more strengths written down in a list. Pin it up somewhere prominent where you'll see it every day - hey, aren't you amazing with all those strengths?

3. Learn to like yourself. You know if you asked one of your friends to explain why they like you so much, it would be embarrassingly flattering. Do you ever recognise that about yourself and like you too? Well now it's time to start doing it and realising that there are many things about you that other people would like to share in - so why are you denying them?
4. Don't conform. You have your own viewpoint, and opinions - maybe even your own unique way of doing something, or a special skill. Show everyone else what that is and don't be afraid for it to be noticed.
5. Focus on other people, so when you go out don't think about yourself for the whole night; notice what other people are like, what they are saying - even whether they seem nervous or not. You will find that there is always someone more nervous or shy than you wherever you go. Help them out, and boost your own sense of capability at the same time.
6. Learn how to control anxiety by breathing exercises, NLP, exercise or thought focussing. Many sports men and women work on tapping routines or thought process routines to channel themselves to achieve their best. It can work for you too, so look into what might work for you and give it a go. Release anxiety through exercise too; find exercises that can help, e.g. Qigong, Yoga.
7. Visualisation can also help overcome shyness. Visualise the event or situation and what causes the shyness or anxiety, and then remodel what happens, a little like the

behaviour modelling in chapter 6. You can restate what will happen in your visualisation and turn it into a moment of serenity and confidence instead.

8. Look into how you can improve your self-image and how you present yourself. Sometimes a 'make-over', for both guys and girls, gives them a whole new outlook and sense of self-appreciation. If nothing else it will revamp a staid and maybe tired old image you may have been carrying around with you for years, and make people take immediate notice.
9. Practice, practice, practice - because you know what they say... And the more often you approach someone new, or do something new, the easier it becomes to do it the next time.
10. Take away the challenge from what you're doing by not having an expectation or a goal - there's an example of taking away the challenge in the little anecdote below.

I went to hear what the dating gurus were saying about it all and here is one of their stories, but in my words (5):

'There was a very shy girl who couldn't bring herself to even talk to anyone she didn't know and the dating guru promised her he could get her talking to any man on any subject by the end of the day. She was sceptical but she agreed to try. Her first challenge was to go up to a man in the street and ask him for the time. She was nervous, but did it - halting and stuttering as she did so. The man simply looked at his watch and told her the time,

before moving swiftly on his way towards the train station entrance.

She came back to the guru, who was looking on.

'Ok, I've done that. What next?'

'Now go and do that another 20 times over,' he said with a smile.

The girl spent the next 30 minutes asking another 20 men the time, and each time she became more relaxed over it, losing the stuttering and even smiling and saying thank you by the end of the task.

'Ok, I've done that - now what? I don't see how this is getting me anywhere. I'm talking to men but not in any useful way.'

'Wait and see,' replied the guru, and then told her the next task. 'Now I want you to ask a man the time and comment on how nice his watch is.'

The girl shrugged her shoulders. She looked around her and spotted a man walking towards her, carrying a briefcase and a rolled up newspaper. She approached him, asked for the time and hurriedly told him he had a nice watch.

'Oh,' he said, slightly mystified and then smiled, nodded and walked on.

'Ok,' she said as she returned to the guru. 'I've done that: now what?'

'Go and do the same thing with another 20 men.' The guru smiled knowingly at her again and gave her a little nod of encouragement. The girl sighed, but did as he told her to. She asked the first 5 men and smiled nicely and walked away. They mainly returned the smile. The next 5 men thanked her back, and she smiled and added another comment like, 'you're welcome', or 'that's ok.' The next 5 men, took a good look at her as she slowed down in her approach and stopped rushing the question and the comments, and the last one of all looked back at her as he walked slowly away. She walked back to the guru again.

'The last one was going to keep talking to me, I think, so I left quickly', she told him, laughing.

'Really? Well that should be your next challenge, then - don't walk away: keep talking back. Tell them you could do with some advice on where to find a really nice watch as it is your brother's birthday coming up soon and you thought it's something he might like. You know the drill, try it on one and then do another 20. I'm going to sit here and get a coffee.' He indicated a little café with chairs and tables outside, and waved her off.

The girl took a deep breath and did as she was told. The same pattern followed. The first few didn't say much more - a few pleasantries, that was all. The next five or so, commented on the weather, and suggested a few local jewellers. But the last one - he came up trumps.

'I have the day off.' He said. I bought mine from a jewellers shop just along here. Would you like me to show you where it is and then maybe I could take you to lunch?' He wasn't tall, dark and handsome, he didn't look amazingly rich, he didn't have a physique like Adonis, but he had a nice smile, a nice manner and was polite. What should she do? She looked across at the guru, who waved bye-bye to her from his table outside the coffee shop.

She went.'

What was the purpose of the exercise?

There was no expectation whenever the girl asked the question. She wasn't waiting for an answer or for something specific to happen. She had no challenge other than just talking, so talking to a stranger gradually lost its ability to cause her anxiety and awkwardness through repetition and the fact that there wasn't a 'cherished outcome' to achieve and be disappointed if she failed in. It was just talking. She talked, she relaxed, she became better at it - and all of a sudden her fear of talking to a stranger was cured.

Now if you work hard at projecting your confidence and destroying your anxiety or awkwardness, you WILL approach someone and then you WILL want to know what to say and how to do it. First of all for the guys, what do women look for?

What women find attractive may be different to what you think…

Shy or sly, tried all the obvious things but still they fail to get the girl? Oddly enough, the things that men find attractive may be quite different to what women find attractive. What are some of the top things that men think they are doing right but cannot impress women at all with?

- Firstly, if you think the richer you are and the more material possessions they have, like a smart car, designer clothes or a fancy apartment, the more instantly impressive you are to women, you are wrong. For some women that may be impressive but more than likely that is not the woman you would be interested in long-term. She is a woman that does not really love you but loves your bank account. I had a date once who worked on precisely this tack. He spent all evening telling me about his Porsche and Merc, his yacht, his holidays in the South of France and his expensive apartment. He carefully displayed his solid gold wristwatch under his designer shirt cuff, and flourished his Gucci wallet at me. Did he ask about anything I did or was interested in during the evening? No. Did he laugh at my joke about my car? He asked if my 'Merc' (the tiniest, least impressive Merc possible: the Mercedes A class) was a convertible and I replied that it would be if you took a tin-opener to its roof. No. And he didn't ask my opinion once either. When he went to the bar to pay the bill, I ran. Did I accept the invitation to a second date? Not on your... He may have been rich but he was boring, self-interested, had no sense of humour - and he had bitten down nails - YUK!

- Next is name dropping, bragging about your important job, or showing how 'clever' you are by being a smart-ass or talking about the important/famous/exciting people you know. Trying to impress a girl by your connections in life doesn't work unless all you want to do is convince her of your wish for a place in next months 'Hello' magazine. Really it indicates how insecure you are. If you have to tell her how wonderful you are in order to get her attention, it sends the wrong message to a girl, and makes you sound arrogant too.

- Then there are the guys with good physiques and who trust that by showing off their muscles they will appeal to women. Ok, girls will admire your six-pack or your spectacular pecs - and then what? There's only so much admiring you can do before you start to wonder when the interesting conversation starts. Just as you think about girls, so they think about guys - *'looks aren't everything…'*

- Cheesy pick-up lines: Generally, when you go to chat up a girl, she never really remembers your initial conversation in detail, but your first approach will give her an impression of the type of person you are. From that she will decide whether to talk to you or not. Those first few words and the way that you come across will make all the difference. Think about who you are, and what you are trying to represent.

- Raise your confidence level and think about how you come across to women in the way you dress, and your appearance. These are the qualities which are going to be more attractive initially than that first ice breaker. If you look naff, at best she'll smile politely and walk away.

So what does work?

The things that impress women are

- The way you approach her and the first impression it gives her of you.
- Your appearance generally.
- Your ability to hold an intelligent and relevant conversation.
- Your courtesy.
- Your interest in what is going on around you and the take you have on it.
- Your good humour.
- Your self-confidence and how you respond and socially interact with the others around you, not just her.
- The passion you have for your interests and beliefs and how you communicate them to her.
- Your self-control around food, drink, other women etc.
- And as importantly, your interest in all those things about her too.

So let's start with the first approach lines:

Ice –breakers or the first approach

- **Introduce yourself** - this almost goes without saying: she's not going to know you exist until you make her aware you're there.
  <u>What to say:</u>
  "I'm Tom, happy to meet you."
  "I'm Tom. I don't believe we've been introduced."

- **Say "hello"** - most women will say it right back, if only because it's common courtesy to do so. However, now you've opened the door to more *conversation* - make sure you have a topic ready to launch into though, otherwise you'll be back to silence in 10 seconds flat!
  What to say:
  "Hi."
  "Hello."

- **Comment on your surroundings** - much less demanding! There's always something around to comment on, wherever you are, so use the environment you're in for an opportunity to comment to her and then gently ease it toward other topics.
  What to say:
  "I've heard this DJ somewhere else; he sounds great."
  "You look like you're having a great day." (Say it with sarcasm if she looks bored or unhappy).

- **Ask an open-ended question** - the hardest part about using an icebreaker is keeping the conversation going and not letting it end 30 seconds after it's begun. You can avoid this by asking a question that requires her to elaborate on her reply, not simply a "yes" or "no."
  What to say:
  "So, what do you do for fun?"
  "So, how do you keep busy at weekends?"

- **Make her smile -** the biggest magic you can work! Women love a man who can make them laugh. It doesn't then seem like a pick-up and it suggests that you are a fun guy to be around.
  What to say:
  "I bet I can make you smile in five seconds." (Have a follow-up or a joke ready though).
  "Want to hear a really bad pickup line?" (Have one ready – here's where you *can* get to use your cheesy one-liners!)

Getting a bit bolder now…

- **Buy her a drink -** in a bar, restaurant or coffee shop, a great icebreaker can simply involve buying her a drink. If you're feeling really smooth, have the waiter take her another round of what she's already having, or if you want to be more aggressive, you could send her your favourite drink accompanied by a cheeky note, with your phone number included. Make sure the waiter tells her who bought her the drink, though - you don't want anyone else capitalising on your entrepreneurial approach! On your way out, stop at her table and introduce yourself - bold but not too invasive.
  What to say:
  "Hope you enjoyed your drink."

"This is my favourite drink; thought you might enjoy it too."

- **Give a sincere compliment** - girls love compliments, but they can work out when the compliment is an insincere one. If you get slapped down, do follow through with a humorous hit back, so that she doesn't believe you're in awe over her, otherwise the game is lost from the start.
  What to say:
  "It's funny that you noticed that… You're very perceptive."
  "You have a nice, cheeky laugh."

Want to be bolder still… Ok, you have been warned that sometimes you may crash and burn with these openers, but life is meant for excitement, isn't it?

- **Ask if she's single** – well you want to know, don't you? Get it over with at the outset. This is quite a bold move but asking a stranger if she's available immediately reveals your intentions and eliminates the chances of awkward misunderstandings.
  What to say:
  "Before I even ask your name, which is probably as beautiful as you are, I need to know - are you single?"
  "Could I be so lucky that you're single?"

- **Be blunt** - even more direct, so put on your bold suit before you attempt this! Walking up to a woman and letting her know you're a decisive guy can be very appealing - even a turn-on (but steel yourself to the possibility of rejection too). She'll probably take your confidence as an indication that you're someone worth talking to.

What to say:

"I was trying to think of a clever pickup line, but then I realised there's no such thing. My name is Tom. What's yours?"

"Would you mind if I joined you?"

Red hot and asking for trouble?

- **Have her buy you a drink** - be cheeky and try some role-reversal. But you've got to be feeling very cheeky and confident for this one:
  What to say:
  "I'll tell you what, how about I let you buy me a drink?"
  "I've always felt that it's a bit chauvinistic to offer to buy a woman a drink. So I'll let you buy me one and promise to repay the favour later."

Now compliments are a tricky thing. As a woman, I've rated them in the 'relatively easy' category because most compliments will be well-received simply because they are a form of flattery, and we all like being flattered. BUT they can also backfire if the compliment is so patently untrue or aimed at simply picking her up, and the lady on the receiving end of it has a sharp brain - and even worse, a sharp tongue! In fact, the right compliment said to a girl could be the difference between making her like you or making her hate you… getting a date or getting rejected… her paying you a compliment back or giving you the finger. Most men give women compliments to try to make them like them, but really you want to give a woman a compliment that makes her notice you and rate you as interesting, observant, intelligent - worth getting to know. For example, you can say:

'You look really hot/pretty/beautiful tonight,' and she will say 'thanks' and treat it as a throwaway line, or you could say something quite different , like:

'Hey, I noticed you standing there and really liked your energy. I knew I'd kick myself if I didn't say hi. My name's Tom, what's yours?'

The reason this works is simple: it's directed at HER and the fact that you've noticed something intrinsically special about her, not just the way she looks. You can also use it as an initial compliment with almost every woman you meet, because their energy is special to them, so it's going to be true for ANY woman you're attracted to. Think about the last five women you've felt physically attracted to. Obviously, you've liked the way they've looked, but there was also something you couldn't quite 'put your finger on' too, wasn't there? That's her 'energy', and that's what you're complimenting.

The other problem with compliments is that they can seem so 'samey' and a woman may well secretly - if not openly - comment that they 'bet you say that to everyone'. The sad truth is most men **don't** regularly make compliments to lots of women in order to chat them up. In fact meeting and trying to chat up just **one** woman makes them so nervous they freeze and forget everything they were going to say, so in desperation they fall back on the same old lines. The trick to a real compliment is to make the recipient feel special.

Once you've used the 'energy' compliment where do you go next? You have to become practised in identifying what it is that makes that person stand out - their 'special' criteria, at that specific moment, that you can comment on. The only way to become practised, is, of course - to practice!

Practice giving people compliments. Set yourself a challenge of at least 5 a day - the people you meet during the day, people in the phone, people on Facebook, people emailing you; anyone just to get into the habit of doing it. It has an initial surprising result - you feel good about yourself too. And it has the same result as the guru's tasks for the girl who couldn't talk to strangers. If you never give compliments, or giving compliments isn't something you're used to, you'll probably feel anxious about doing it, and then it's hard to do. On the other hand, if you are someone who gives compliments all the time, it usually means that you are happy, that you feel good about yourself, and life feels good too. You can actually reverse engineer anxiety and unhappiness this way. You can become happier and feel better about yourself simply by giving more compliments.

If you want to be good with women, you've also got to remove the fear of being needy and many men equate showing a softer side to women - a romantic side - with being needy. It's not. It's simply expressing something that most women will respond enthusiastically to. Romantic compliments come not from a place of need, but from a place of personal strength and women recognise that strength in a man who is brave enough to make her a romantically inspired compliment at the appropriate moment. How to make that compliment special to her? Simply think about what it is about that woman that is special right now, and focus on that.

I've been addressing all the openers and ice-breakers to the guys so far, but of course any of them could be used by the pro-active lady, it's just the tradition is for the guys to make the first approach and as I perceive I may want to meet a 'shy guy', I need to give the guys the strategy to succeed too. There are plenty of ideas about how to strike up that all-important conversation either way, so girls, help yourself too.

Finally for the guys - the insider knowledge all men want: how women fall in love...'

Women fall in love with a man who 'gets' them on a deep, emotional level, and they call this a 'bond' or a 'connection' between them. She never falls out of love, even if she tries to hide it. (This is why you see so many beautiful, amazing women stuck with loser boyfriends, or even in abusive relationships.) Making a woman fall in love with you takes a variety of different things - from the conversations you have, to the dates you go on, right down to the sex (See chapter 11 and sex). But the real 'trick' to making a woman love you is simple. You have to figure out what makes her unique, and then talk to her in a such a way as to let her know you 'get' her uniqueness. Well we're all unique, aren't we? So isn't that easy once you get to know someone? It would seem so, but here are the ways you could screw it up.

Mistake number 1: Trying to bribe your way into her heart

Expensive dates…
Bouquets of red roses…
Holidays to her favourite, faraway place…
Sadly no amount of money can help you buy love.

'So how come rich guys are so successful with women?' You ask. The simple answer is they're not. Rich guys get lots of sex, because they spend as much as they like to get it - and there will always be breed of woman who is happy to oblige. A little aside here for some more of Pete's worst date tales:

- ❖ The one who asked him if he could lend her £170,000 on their first date, but lost interest when he said no.
- ❖ The ones - and apparently there were quite a few - who would go on a date with anyone because they knew it was practice for the guy to pay on the first date - then there wasn't a second one…
- ❖ I also quite enjoyed the one who was a psychotherapist and told him she didn't think they were suited but gave him her card for professional purposes at the end of a date - but that's just my sense of humour!

However, when it comes to long-term, lasting relationships, lots of very wealthy men end up very lonely. In fact, a much higher percentage of wealthy men have MULTIPLE divorces than lower-income men, simply because the women mainly married them for their money. So keep your wallet in your pocket and the bribery in the bank.

Mistake number 2: Too many compliments

"You look great!"
"I love that dress on you!"
"Wow, that's so cool!"

On an average date, the average woman can get up to fifty compliments from just one man. Supposing you reduced your normal first date down to just one hour, and included the time you spend eating, almost every other sentence would be, 'wow…' Find out what she's really like, as a person, and once you find out something she doesn't tell *every* guy she dates, your well-timed, appropriate, specific compliment will make her heart flutter.

Mistake number 3: Treating all women exactly the same way

You may think you treat every woman as a unique person but how often have you said something to a woman because you think the stereotype of 'woman' likes it - my last girlfriend liked this, or don't all women laugh at…? Sadly, this will ring warning bells to her even though you don't think you're doing it and she will think you want her only for her body, or only because she has a pretty face, and not because of who she really is.

Get to know your girl's 'type' before you date her. Her 'type' - isn't that stereotypical again? No, it's establishing the things that make her absolutely unique and therefore how you're going to respond to her to determine what you need to do to make her fall in love with you.

Finally a few more things that men should know about women:

1. Persistence is flattering... But if she's not smitten, it then becomes annoying, and finally, downright creepy. Quit while you're ahead, if she doesn't give you any encouragement.

2. Women's lib doesn't include going 'dutch'.

3. Women love a man who talks about his family. It means he cares - and even more importantly, it means he might one day be into having one of his own.

4. Women love a man with a plan... So don't umm and ahh your way through things and leave her to decide.

6. Women don't want men to solve all their problems... they just want them to listen sometimes.

7. She knows when you're lying. According to some research, 'women's intuition' is real: It stems from the mothers ability to read her baby's needs by observing facial expressions and vocal patterns – so don't.

8. Thank you goes a long way. If you remember to say 'thank you', even if you're not pulling your weight in the relationship, she'll put up with it for a lot longer than if you don't.

9. Women still like being asked out on a date properly…

10. Women prefer macho to date and sensitive to marry. Men can actually dictate the types of women they attract by how much they express their masculine side or their sensitive one. Now that's called clever commitment- dodging!

11. Women like spontaneity, but whisking her away on a surprise weekend trip is spontaneous, showing up fifteen minutes late without any money and suggesting you stay in with a DVD isn't.

12. She is less excited about receiving lingerie than you are about giving it. If it's a present for her - is this not in reality a present for you? Choose something *she'll* appreciate rather than you.

13. Cleaning and doing the dishes… Is one of the sexiest things you can for her - earn yourself some brownie points, do!

14. Sexual appetite in women increases with age: as women mature, they become more comfortable with their bodies. The young, 'hot' women in sexy attire are often self-conscious and unadventurous in bed, but older woman are less inhibited. Mmm, now that's set you thinking, hasn't it?

15. Even independent women are attracted to caring men: Even a self-sufficient and independent career woman still likes to feel protected and provided for on some level.

16. You can't expect her to be in better shape than you are.
Men tend to be more visual than women, so a woman may be more inclined to forgive her mate's imperfect physical attributes. But if a man sets store by their partner's physical appearance, it is only fair he returns the favour by being comparably attractive, or taking care of himself.

Now it's the ladies turn and finding out some of those male secrets:

Knowledge is power, so use it well:

1. Earning money makes men feel valuable. If a woman loses a job, she pragmatically goes out to find another one. If a man loses his job, his ego suffers a greater blow than his wallet, initially.

2. Men like to fix things. There's a difference between this and the routine tasks of washing up and hovering. Men like tasks where they can use a bit of ingenuity and show off their brawn, like putting up a shelf or unblocking the sink. Play to his ego by asking for his help in your 'bigger' projects. He'll happily turn up with work box in hand to show off his DIY skills.

3. Men like to drive because they don't think women are good drivers, and they need to feel in control. Give him the chance to get behind the wheel and he'll feel empowered and much less of a back-seat driver!

4. When you give men space, they appreciate you more. Men need alone time and also male bonding time. It's been called going into their cave and various other kinds of things but if you make sure he gets it, it will make the time you have together more valued by him.

5. Men do look at other women, no matter how happy they are. If your man isn't subtle in this area, wheel in the modelling and use those mirror neurons and carefully scripted phrases to make the standard of the behaviour required of him VERY obvious, so hopefully your man is subtle in this area. This doesn't mean that your man is going to cheat on you or act on it with more than a smile… but its male instinct to look.

6. When they are sick they LOVE to be babied - time to get maternal and for once he'll LOVE it.

7. Funnily enough, they love flowers and chocolates - it shows you appreciate them too.

8. They hate talking on the phone, so if he does he must REALLY like you…

Attraction for a man is based on a combination of visual chemistry (V1), perceived challenge (C1) and perceived value (V2) in order to make a deep and lasting connection (C2). It could read as a formula:

$$V1 + C1 + V2 = C2$$ - easy to remember isn't it?

Visual chemistry (V1) separates friendship from a relationship - you fancy as well as like them.
Challenge (C1) makes them worth winning - you never value something you're simply given.
Value (V2) is what makes you in demand - unique, not easy to duplicate.
Connection (C2) is what turns the attraction and liking into a lasting relationship.

And the big one – what makes a man fall in love?

- Responding to the feminine in a woman.
- Finding a role for himself in her life - a supportive role, a protective role, and a necessary role.
- Feeling he can simply be himself with her -whatever that is for him.
- Despite his protective role, also feeling like he isn't going to be smothered, censured or controlled by her.
- Understanding where she is coming from and that it does not threaten him, or his need for freedom to choose, decide for himself - even be laddish with his mates.

There are **7** basic traits that every guy and girl is looking for initially in their potential partner:

1. Playfulness
2. Confidence
3. Femininity/masculinity
4. Integrity/class
5. Spontaneity
6. Independence
7. Sexual attractiveness/chemistry

Beyond that there are a further **5** additional traits that will turn a date into a mate:

1. Nurturing
2. Contentedness
3. Loyalty
4. Dependence/and interdependence
5. Appreciation

But these come AFTER you've established the strong attraction with the initial 7.

Sexuality is the feminine as opposed to the masculine - or the masculine as opposed to the feminine. You have to be very aware of the oppositeness of your potential partner to feel sexual chemistry. The masculine side of a man is attracted to the feminine energy of the woman in equal proportion to their own masculine energy - and vice versa. A man is always looking for the feminine energy of a woman to complement them, as is a woman looking for the masculine energy of a man. Allow that to be apparent in your dealings with any potential date, and you'll stay out of the dreaded friends' zone. If a man offers to help you, the woman, don't emasculate him by declaring your independence and how you don't need men. Let him help you… A woman being able to accept help from a man is still a show of her inner strength, in that she doesn't have to try to prove herself. In our modern world of equality, it is all too easy to use our ability and skills as a barrier to allowing someone access to our softer side. The capable woman lawyer needs to show herself to be unassailable in court, but she needn't be so in her private life. Women are increasingly finding themselves in environments where they are in control and playing out the 'masculine' role. A man still wants to see a woman in a feminine role in her personal life, so if he offers to pay the bill, well…

Men: be brave enough to offer a romantic compliment to a woman - it's being able to respond to her emotively from a strong sense of yourselves - and I'm emphasising the word 'strong' here. Don't be afraid to respond to her femininity, or show you have emotions and vulnerabilities too. She will think much more of you if you do.

Chapter 8: A little bit of conversation

So was it time for the first proper night out, employing all the strategy ideas so far and to find out what happens next? I decided It was time for me to try putting all the strategies together, but I knew I couldn't test them out on Pete this time. He was starting to notice that my behaviour pattern was different from one date to the next and his confusion was apparent. Apart from that, so was mine, because I was testing these ideas out on him yet wasn't sure now if I now still wanted to attract him! I needed some real life lab rats - or maybe bar rats might do - and then I could catalogue the responses. Pete would remain my 'control experiment' - poor Pete! So off I went, with my best friend Mandy, eager to see if what I had developed so far worked. Our test tonight: to bar-crawl central London and test out our ice breakers, our complimenting ritual, our pro-active approach, establishing our place as women of high value - even trying a bit of behaviour modelling, and then, having gathered as many numbers as we could, to test out the best text, phone and email responses. Wow - we had our work cut out; better get on with it.

    Stop number one was into a bar in Oxford Circus, fairly early evening but it was already loud and full. In we walked with our pro-active approach in mind, excited and hyped up to test out the theories; be in the moment and create an initial presence. I told myself off; slow down. Stand in your spotlight. So we did - literally! I stopped dead at the top of the stairs to the lower level bar and surveyed the scene below - a little kind of 'hello, here I am!' Several male heads turned and we held up the rest of the crowd thronging behind us to get in.

'Move on please miss,' said the bouncer politely, but firmly.

'Of course,' I swung round and smiled at him - full beam charm - and he smiled back. A couple more heads turned, and one or two men at the back of the crowd jostling behind me craned their heads to see WHO was it that the bouncer was allowing to hold up the flow? Ah - celebrity status already! We made our way forward, smiling and saying 'hi' to everyone within shouting distance, and at the bar, spoke directly to the guy either side as we were ordering drinks. Then we departed, making sure that as we moved around later, working the room, the ones we'd greeted on arrival got a 'hello you again' as we did a return pass.

Strategy principles so far:

- Be in the moment and take your time, don't rush: establish your 'celebrity status as soon as you arrive, survey the room and make your entrance. You WILL be noticed.
- Arrive in a positive, high-energy state.
- Smile.
- Be proactive/ interactive with everyone.

- Follow up short interactions with a repeat to reinforce the connection - it may develop later.

In we went, still smiling and as soon as we reached the bottom of the stairs, there was a group of guys watching our arrival.

'Hi there, love the shirt!' I approached the nearest one who was wearing a Cath Kidston style shirt. Cath Kidston, would you believe? I was actually quite envious, but I stopped myself from examining it further and examined him instead. As I commented on the shirt, I lightly touched his inner arm just above the elbow. There was a visible frisson from him and his eyes locked on me.

'My sister chose it for me - she said I might pull with it.' He looked hopefully at me and I winked back.

'Who knows,' I replied playfully, and started to move on to the next group a little further along the bar, where Mandy had taken up residence: time to play the group game. I made sure I looked back teasingly at Cath Kidston and he watched me walk along the bar, film star wiggle and all. Before I left he'd palmed me his business card with his mobile written on the back, and a clever little comment.

'Do give me a call - you could help me choose a better shirt...'

That was worthy of me - he was a fast learner. I made a mental note of it, was this those little mirror neurons working already?

Strategy principles deployed successfully:

- Flirt moves - the film star wiggle, the touch and the backwards look.
- Teasing opener and playful response.
- Moving on quickly to the next opportunity.
- Having no expectations, just talking.
- Having fun.

Mandy was working it hard with her group so I joined in. I thought of the most ridiculous thing to stay to start the games off the games.

'There are two men just over there stalking me - and one is FBI. Would you be my bodyguard?' The poor guy I said this to was completely fazed for a moment, until he realised it was a game and played along nicely.

'Oh, of course, do I have to fight them off or just protect you from them?'

'Either would be fine - but it would mean you would have to stay close to me all evening.'

'Its' a tough job,' he sighed, 'but someone's got to do it...' We both laughed, and then introduced ourselves. He was actually very nice and we had some fun with the role play game for a little while. We started to talk more seriously after the first five minutes of hilarious double-talk and I established some of his hobbies weren't a million miles different to mine. He asked if I was busy at the weekend, and I told him about my family commitments. He reciprocated by telling me a little about his too. There was some rapport starting to grow between us until

Mandy signalled it was time to move on - we had WORK to do, so we swopped numbers again , and off we went once more.

Strategy principles in action:

- Having fun.
- Using role play to create conversation.
- Moving on intermittently – not letting the conversation get stale.
- Playfulness.
- Establishing your values.
- Establishing their values.

The evening was a hub-bub of ice breakers, flirting, exchanged numbers and conversational practice - fascinating in its own way, and gathering us no end of contacts to try out phase two of the conversational aspect of the plan out on our collection of lab rats.

Some of the best ice breakers we learnt or tested out were these:

Creating sexual tension:

Girl: It's cold.
Guy: Yes it is.
Girl: You're not allowed to be cold - you're a guy (big teasing smile).
Guy: You're so mean... leaving the door wide open for a lot of flirting.

Good ways to start the conversation:

- ✓ Ask a favour.
- ✓ Ask a direction.
- ✓ Give a compliment.
- ✓ Ask for help with...
- ✓ Role play nonsense – see the body guard line.
- ✓ Are you Polish, French, a Russian spy… anything to elicit a strong response.
- ✓ Asking a fantasy question - If you could just go anywhere in the world tomorrow, where would you go? Or - If you could do a job you hated for a £100000 a year or a job you loved for £10000, which would you choose?
- ✓ Create sexual tension with your question - 'Oh dear, it's never going to work between us!' and a wink. You create a wonderful perceived challenge then as the guy/girl desperately wants to prove you wrong.
- ✓ Create a tease - for example where there is a particularly popular guy, you would otherwise be battling for his attention. Instead, remove yourself from the throng by saying - 'it's crazy you have all these women flocking round you; how does it feel to have them all think you're so good looking?' The implication is that YOU don't - a challenge if ever there was one, and one which IMMEDIATELY singles YOU out as different!

- ✓ Ask person-related questions - what's the least cool or geekiest thing about you? -what's the best thing about your job? FOLLOW UP: 'So what would be the best question to ask a...? Then they have to follow up too and keep the conversation flowing.

Useful teasing touches (to accompany the ice-breakers):

Male and female targets-

- The inside forearm - quick and light and as if to misdirect.
- Inside the back or the waist.
- On the back, just under the shoulder blades.
- Smell his aftershave or her perfume.
- Quick touch to the knee - if sitting.

Male targets only-

- The nape of the neck.
- Around the ears - but don't linger.
- Back of the hand to the chest or stomach (definitely not on a girl!).

- A little tease and then followed up with a 'sorry!' and a quick kiss on the cheek when he complains.

So we eventually went home with a swag bag of phone numbers and even some email addresses off business cards. Now stage 2 of the conversational strategy could be developed. To text: or not to text? That is the question LOL. Texting is really difficult to get right. It's a few words only, but they have to imply the right meaning and sense otherwise you lose the impact completely. Texts should be:

➢ For information/confirmation.
➢ For logistics - arranging a time place, arrival time etc.
➢ For entertainment - a short snappy comment.
➢ Throwing a comment 'out there' but not designed to require a response.
➢ Concise.
➢ Short.

When a text is for information gathering or logistics, it is entirely to establish the where and when - or to confirm the where and when or advise on a change of plan, late arrival or so on. It never needs a response other than a factual one otherwise you come across as needy. So if you are meeting someone you don't know well, or a blind date, texting something like:

'I'm running a bit late. Meet you at the bar in ten minutes - where are you standing?' is fine. It informs them of timing, and shows a directness and confidence that suggest you will be interesting to meet even though you are going to be a bit late. But texting:

'I'm running a bit late. Are you there already because I don't like going into a bar and not knowing where to find someone...' is not. It says you have no confidence in yourself - and you are late too: not an attractive prospect!

How about the text for entertainment or encouragement? It needs to be a short, snappy comment because you want to make an impact. Texting is more about tone than timing. Whatever you text, it needs to convey your high value status. Here were some of our most effective ones in establishing a first date invitation:

1. His question: 'Are you around this weekend?'

2. Strategy response: 'Yes, first one in ages.'

3. His next question: 'That's great - would you like to do something?'

The rationale?

If you texted back, 'yes, would you like to do something?' at stage 2, he would be left with the impression that you are just waiting to be asked = low value.

Implying that you're nearly always busy, and he's been lucky catching you when you're unexpectedly free = high value because you're obviously in demand.

Here's another successful exchange:

Throwing a comment 'out there' but not designed to require a response: If you're already involved with someone you like, don't ask for their validation - that is needy. Simply make your own statement.

'I miss you,' is a high value statement text. However if you texted:

'Do you miss me?' it is low value.

<u>The rationale?</u> *'Do you miss me?* Is needy, and actually demeans your value, whereas making your statement and not needing a response says *I'm confident enough in myself to tell you what I'm thinking without needing you to respond...* Message received?

- ❖ **Never** invest in how attractive you find the person as it is quite likely more than the investment they've earned. If they've made no effort, why would you chase after them? They haven't earned your time or involvement yet.
- ❖ **Never** read any meaning into 'xxx' or no x's: Neither implies anything other than that it's the way this person signs themselves off.
- ❖ **Never** assume with anyone. Get certainty. If they haven't called you, don't make excuses for them - 'they're busy', or 'maybe they didn't get the first text', or 'maybe they lost my number ' If you liked them enough to still want to know if they are interested in you or not, here's the way to do it:

Send this text at around 9pm on a night when you are out somewhere interesting:

> 'The music (or whatever you want to comment on) here is awesome - you should come (or) why aren't you here too?'

Why? For the following reasons:

1. It's too late for them to get there so you create demand without them easily being able to obtain what you're telling them about - it makes them think they're missing out.
2. It also says, *'I'm out and I have a fantastic life - look what you're missing out on.'*
3. There is no question mark so it is a statement. It is therefore confident and justifies 2. - you don't need them there, you are simply pointing out they're missing something awesome.

Being confident and certain about yourself and what you do is very sexy. This message will say to its recipient, *this is me and I am awesome* - as well as the music/meal or whatever it is you've commented on. If they respond, then you need to continue the high value repartee.

If the reply is, *'you didn't invite me'* or something similar, remain playful and send something like, *'you should have known - you're in my bad books again now',* and a wink or a smiley icon to show you're teasing.

Suppose the reply is *'I can't come tonight - are you around at the weekend?'* Go back to the message above, *'I am actually - first free one in ages...'*

If they don't respond, you know they're really not interested in you and so you move on. No investment in you = no investment in them. Believe me, it worked a treat with our contacts. Probably the best response was the guy who apologised for being unable to text as he'd been in a car accident just afterwards and had broken his arm and leg and was in traction in hospital. Bless him, he got the nurse to text back in the end - and then of course we had a whole new role play situation to play with!

> ❖ **Never stand on ceremony** until you have certainty. You can unnecessarily burn all your bridges all at once. Remember we are all different and have different constraints on our time, availability and inclination to get involved. A shy guy will need a little encouragement. A shrinking violet needs to be asked. If a guy takes your number and doesn't ring you, he might genuinely have been too busy to get round to it. Men compartmentalise things so until he's in a social/flirting situation again, the 'work' head might have taken over and made him forget. They also may not be that into **yet,** but that isn't necessarily a reflection on whether they **could** be attracted. Persistence can be its own reward, so don't be so arrogant as to stand on ceremony and get stroppy. Get certainty instead.
>
> ❖ **Never become obsessed** with one potential contact or date. Fill your time with other activities, other interests,

other dates. Remember the investment rule - invest in them what they invest in you.

Texting is only one part of the communication checklist. Rapport is created in many ways and the key to it all is balance - and spreading it around through as many media as you are comfortable with.

Next come emails.

Emails can be as tricky as texts - and are what anyone who internet dates has to tangle with initially. How do you imply you're high value when you're telling someone all about you in order to try to tempt them in? Here are some rules I came up with after a spell of testing out the internet waters too:

- ✓ If you get a reply, it has to be a proper one - not a one-liner.
- ✓ If they can't spell or have poor grammar, unless it really doesn't bother you, translate that into the way they might speak…
- ✓ If they don't reply for days on end then do the same yourself - remember the investment rule.
- ✓ It's ok to send the first message or wink, but if they don't respond, don't chase after them - remember the investment rule.
- ✓ Be playful in the same way that you would be if actually talking to them, but also make sure your high value status remains intact.
- ✓ Don't tell them more than they need to know before meeting you - too much information is off-putting. Where is the mystery if they know all about you before meeting?

- ✓ Establish their principles and values are in line with yours in the same way as if you were meeting them and holding a conversation.
- ✓ Never offer more than you are being given, so here are two examples of emails showing what would be good to establish values, and what is bad...

To the guy who keeps cancelling dates, delaying or just squeezing you in, slip this in instead:

Good: *'I did my best to come up with a plan, all you had to do was come up with a date - you really must try harder (winking icon)...!'*

You've stated your principles, been certain in what you want, but also been slightly playful - in a kind of 'must try harder' way.

Bad: *'I did my best to come up with a plan, all you had to do was come up with a date - you really must try harder (winking icon)! I don't mind waiting until next week if that's easier, or I'm free at the weekend - so we could do both...'*

The second example has made the point that he needs to put in more effort - and then ruined it all by being 'available' whenever he chooses. She's created no demand at all, and so her value has sunk to low (sad icon).

Lastly, not quite as good as the face to face meeting, but a good interim measure - and more important that texting or emailing: the phone. Pretend you are talking to them face to face and then you will sound natural, but remember the golden rules of chatting:

- ☒ Don't sit at home when there's nothing else to do - be already in a rush.
  - ✓ Having a divided focus so there's a time limit YOU impose on the conversation makes you more enigmatic and therefore creates demand.
  - ✓ Having a clearly stated deadline for when you must go increases the value of the time you're giving them.
  - ✓ When you finish the phone call, do be proactive about arranging something else - *'I've got to go now, but I'm around over the weekend if you want to catch up again...'*

Funnily enough, I couldn't quite bring myself to test out the theories on Mr Bodyguard - or at least, not until they'd been honed to perfection, and then they went like this:

Texts:

Him: Hi, how are you today?

Me: Nice to hear from you. I'm fine today, thanks.

Him: Not in need of a bodyguard still, maybe?

Me: Well, it's funny you should ask…

Him: I am available for bodyguard duties when asked…

Me: A second income then? But I might not be able to afford your rates whilst I'm on the run.

Him: I could waive my fee as a bonus offer for you?

Me: That's sweet of you. I'll sign you up then.

Him: Are you free at the weekend?

Me: Well actually I am - the first free one in ages.

Him: Can I call you later to arrange something?

Me: I'll take off my Mata Hari costume so you can ring me this evening (wink).

Him: Great - talk later.

On the Phone:

Him: Hi - is it safe to talk?

Me: Only if you've made sure the phone's not bugged your end.

Him: No it's quite safe! You are one cheeky lady - do you always sign men up as your bodyguards?

Me: Only if I think they would make a good one-– I have very exacting standards.

Him: I'd better know what they are then, so I can make sure I'm up to scratch!

Me: There's quite a list but I will coach you in them if you need that.

Him: Now it's you signing me up - where's the dotted line?

Me: Ah well, I need to do interviews in person though - you may be fine on paper but fail in other ways…

Him: Well that's perfect because then I can ask you out for a drink at the weekend and do my interview then. Would that work for you?

Me: Well that would be fine because ironically you've caught me at the one time I can say yes for once.

We arranged the date…

Chapter 9: Rejection isn't a dirty word

Of course when I was out and about collecting numbers on my bar crawl for lab rats with Mandy, I got rejected a number of times. I'd already steeled myself for this before I went and had done a lot of thinking about rejection because for most of us, rejection IS a dirty word. It makes you feel useless, unattractive, uninteresting and ultimately, unwilling to put yourself through it again. Yet rejection is only a form of a mistake and we are told to try, try, try again when we make a mistake, aren't we? *Practice makes perfect* is another neat little response. *Persistence wins the race* - they're all true and all we really need to do is understand the things that make us vulnerable to the bad feelings that rejection create in us and try to defuse the ticking bomb before it goes off and splatters egg all over our face.

The only thing we should all know about rejection is that it happens all the time. So what's the big deal?

The only people who find rejection difficult are the ones who think they shouldn't be rejected. And why should rejection be such a problem? Rejection only becomes a problem if you make it one by valuing the outcome of a situation so much that to fail in any way is devastating. Think of all these silly assumptions that we build up around the outcome of something:

'But s/he's so hot. I'll be gutted if they say no….'

'If this one goes wrong there is no hope for me.'

'Why don't they like me – is there something wrong with me?'

'There must be an easier way than this…'

'I don't want them to think I'm desperate or needy…'

'Why does it always happen to me?'

'Being rejected is so awful, I don't want it to happen to me again.'

'There are people out there who don't have to go through all this…'

Rejection and being rejected is simply a matter of the way we think and if we change the way we think about something, we change our response too.

So why do we fear rejection and what creates a sense of rejection in us? Well there are a number of reasons but they're all linked to one basic issue - thinking that the outcome of whatever we felt rejected by mattered so much, that it was irreplaceable. Apart from life itself - and a few art treasures or endangered species - is anything really that irreplaceable? Especially if it's only a potential date who you haven't even got to know yet? So I set out to replace those rejection phrases in my head before I even walked out the door. I came up with this reasoning instead:

'But s/he's so hot, I'll be gutted if they say no…'

- ❖ We fool ourselves into thinking that a person we are approaching or are attracted to really matters. How much are you over-valuing that person WITHOUT EVEN KNOWING THEM? The next time you see someone you think is really hot, remind yourself that:
    - They may not even sound nice.
    - They may not actually be nice.
    - They may have completely different principles and values to you.
    - You actually may even actively dislike them.

Stop valuing them as anything other than someone who is initially physically attractive to you. They have an awful lot more to prove before you start to value them. If you tell yourself all of that before you approach them, they are no longer the important prize to win, which makes you so nervous and so anxious of rejection. They simply become another person to ask the time of, like the girl following the dating guru's advice.

'If this one goes wrong there is no hope for me.'

- ❖ Why is that? How many things *must* work out right now? Did your career materialise overnight? Your qualifications? Did you suddenly earn all the money to buy your house in one hit? If you lost your life savings, it might matter this much. Even if you lost your job, it would be pretty dire - but if you are rejected by one potential date? Surely there is the potential for another one standing right next to them at the bar, or in the supermarket, or at the gym, or... isn't there? **Intent** is what builds pressure, but if there is no intent, there is no pressure. When was the last time you had a bad meal and gave up eating?

'Why don't they like me — is there something wrong with me?'

- ❖ There are types we like and types we don't. Some people like them tall and skinny, some short and dainty, some dark-haired, some bald, some sporty, some geeky. So what if they don't like you? Maybe you're simply not their type, but that doesn't mean there's anything wrong with you. In fact for every person whose type you aren't, there will be a corresponding person where you most definitely ARE, and yet the person standing next to you isn't. Does that person keep saying 'what's wrong with me?'

Don't fall into the trap of thinking that everyone must like you to make you feel secure. If you try to please everyone you will risk compromising or diluting your standards and beliefs, because theirs may not be the same as yours, and you will become average to everyone. Be what and who you are and be extraordinary to someone. It only takes one!

'I don't want them to think I'm desperate or needy…'

- ❖ Whatever you project is what people will assume about you. Every day someone gets the wrong impression about someone else. As you dither about whether to talk to them or not, that person is already starting to make some assumptions about you, or talking to someone else instead. Risk communicating with them and showing them the real you - and why should that be desperate or needy if you aren't?

'Why does it always happen to me?'

- But it happens to everyone else too - hadn't you noticed? Look around you next time you're out and notice who else is trying and maybe being rejected, and then simply trying again.

'Being rejected is so awful, I don't want it to happen to me again.'

- It is far easier to live through the pain of a single moment - like a small pinch, whereas going all thorough your life feeling discontented because you never find what you're looking for is like a dull ache that continues interminably.

'There are people out there who don't have to go through all this...'

- No there aren't - everyone suffers some form of rejection at some point in their life. Pain is always relative to the label and meaning of the situation. Why not think of it as an embarrassing or amazing story to tell instead?

Some ways to dilute the importance you give to any situation:

Don't focus on the results; focus on what you do to get them.

        Results are irrelevant, because

      Effort is what counts.

    Just because they say no,

      Expect nothing to be so important that you

        Can't have another go at it, and

          Treat it all as a learning curve...

Fear of rejection is one of the biggest barriers to getting out there and making it happen for yourself. Don't make it one you can't get past by overvaluing the results until you know the results are worth having.

And the last word - here's a great line to leave with if you want to avoid the risk of being rejected face to face.

'Here's my number - if we get on over the phone, perhaps we can do something more.' Give them your card and then go. No chance at all of rejection there...

Chapter 10: The pleasure/pain principle & other advanced techniques

'Success is a science, if you have the conditions, you get the results.' Oscar Wilde.

Ever heard of Pavlov's dogs? Most of us have. Pavlov was a psychologist who trained dogs to salivate at the sound of a bell because they came to associate it with being fed and that was their expectation when they heard the bell ring. Now of course we aren't dogs, even if you have occasionally been called 'a sly dog', or far worse - 'a right bitch' - but we do have a similarity to them. Like all living, reasonably sentient beings, we repeat what is pleasant and avoid what was unpleasant. So here we go with the pleasure/pain principle - the first in the more advanced techniques aimed at getting the guy or grabbing the girl.

Have you noticed the same thing I have about Pete? The more interesting I become just **as me**, the more interested he becomes **in** me. I wondered if the pleasure pain principle would work the final magic. Here's the tale I heard which made me work it out in the first place - the same very clever dating guru as before (5).

'A guy was just out of a serious relationship and feeling a bit down. He wasn't looking but ironically he met another really attractive, interesting, funny sweet girl. She was so nice, he couldn't resist going on a date with her, and he liked her. He went on another date, and liked her more. He went on a third date but then the little voice inside every guy that undermines his inclination to get involved, put its foot in it too.

"Hey, you've only just got out of one situation - you don't want to immediately jump into another one, do you?"

He thought about it and decided he didn't. He was still stinging from the rejection after his breakup and he didn't want to risk going through that again - or at least not quite as soon as this. 'I'll tell her I don't want anything serious - that will sort it out,' he told himself. So he did just that. He went on the date and told her at the end of it that she was really nice, and he liked her, but he didn't want a relationship with her.

Now what would be your normal reaction to that, girls - or mine? It would be to feel rejected and hurt - our pride hurt possibly more than our feelings, and to question what was wrong with us. Was there anything wrong with the girl? No, actually he liked her and found her really attractive, interesting, funny and sweet. The problem was in his head, not with her. So, did she react rejected, cross, or angry? No, she did a REALLY smart thing and set the pleasure/pain principle in motion instead.

"That's fine," she replied. "I'm not asking you to marry me." She gives him a really nice kiss and goes. He drives home wondering why she isn't pissed off at him. It plays on his mind and periodically he goes back to it and continues to wonder. In his head he is thinking, "that was a nice kiss," but his brain is now scrambled. Now he feels as if he may have been over-reactive but she hadn't dropped her affection level and hadn't got cross - in fact she didn't seem affected at all. Now he feels a bit like a drama queen, and she's the cool girl. All he'd really meant was that he liked her but he hadn't wanted to lose his freedom by making a commitment to her right now. He wonders now exactly why he felt the need to say anything so awkward at all.

Days passed and the guy thought about the girl some more. She was very nice, and he was at a loose end so he decided to call her. She was pleased to hear from him and friendly and encouraging but to his, "would you like to do something?" she was unfortunately busy, but she 'was around' next week.

"When?"

"Maybe Thursday."

"Would you like to do something then?"

"Ok."

They meet on Thursday but unfortunately she only has 'an hour or so' for him and cuts the date short. On the date she is lovely - she's fun, she looks amazing, she's playful, sexy and she ends it with another amazing kiss. The guy starts to associate only good things with her. He asks for another date and she's busy again until later next week. They go out again, but again she only has a short time to spend with him. On the date, once again she's so much fun and the kiss at the end of it makes him think he wants more than just an hour of her time every week or so, when she's free. He backtracks and says it.

"Remember how I said I didn't want a relationship with you? Well, this is really embarrassing but I was wrong..." '

The clever girl applied all the principles I have been establishing so far and added the pleasure/pain tool to them to achieve a complete turn-around. She:

- He established herself as fun, proactive, and interesting - all the things that are attractive.
- She made it quite clear she was high value by being busy and limiting her available time for the guy to when it suited her in her own on-going lifestyle.
- She invested only as much in him as he did in her, so even though he said he didn't want a relationship, when he asked her out, she allowed him **limited** access to her time in return.
- She didn't over-react, or get over-emotional when he said he didn't want a relationship. She accepted it calmly - she understood that guys find emotional reactions off-putting and complicated. Instead of trying to deal with them they will usually just walk away.
- She stated her case, without even having to state it by the way she was only available sometimes and for short periods.
- She didn't write him off straightaway, she treated him as not being interested in a relationship **yet...**

- She framed his behaviour for him so he anticipated the time spent with her would be fun, and of course, then it was.
- She left him wanting more, and was independent, and confident in herself in getting on with her own life. That was 'sexy' for him, because the thing he was concerned about - commitment - wasn't even an issue for her so the threat was taken away from the situation for him.
- She didn't over-value the situation or him by being upset when he said he didn't want a relationship. She took the pressure off in fact by responding, 'ok, if that's not what you want, then that's not what you want.' She only placed as much value on their interaction as he did. In fact she relegated him in her priorities, whereas when we feel like we are trying to persuade someone to do something, we escalate them in our priorities and give them far more attention than they deserve. Then rejection hurts.
- Finally, the girl saw the guy on HER TERMS and showed him why he would want a relationship whilst in fact he got less and less of her time. You always want more of what you can't have - especially if it's nice…

It's often not so much what we do but how we react to what is done that establishes an outcome. The girl in the story induced the guy to anticipate only pleasure from her, not pain, therefore he wanted more. If she had been a drama queen, he would have wanted no more at all. Apply the pleasure, reduce the pain - ALWAYS.

Girls, remember the fundamental principle for finding the right guy? You want a man who adores you, but that means you have to be adorable too. Guys, you want a girl to adore: the same principle applies either way, doesn't it?

Girls defy the stereotype of the woman who is over-emotional, over-reactive and over-demanding. Be calm, rational and value yourself: then he will value you too. Guys, look for the girl who projects that.

Of course the pleasure/pain principle is only one of many you can employ to get you on the right route to where you want to be, and there are many stops we make to check the route, and B roads we follow by mistake along the way. What happens when it's all going perfectly and then that road block the police just set up earlier stops you in your tracks? Well continuing the analogy, you'd take another route to your destination. That's exactly what the girl did with the guy when she employed the pleasure/pain principle, but there are some other common snags you can come across, and I hit them several times over on my bar trawl and on my dates with Pete.

Embarrassed because you want their phone number but have already forgotten their name?

- ❖ Waving your phone at them playfully, say, 'what's your name again?' They'll say their Christian name, and you respond, 'no, not your first name - I've already got that on my phone - your last name…'

Feeling like it's all going wrong? Slow it down and add tension.

- ❖ Slow things down yourself. Charisma is all about taking control and controlling the tempo: linger on things that work and dictate the pace. For example they are about to move on without swapping numbers, you create more tension and pull them back by introducing a playful false debt, 'I can't believe you just… Now you owe me…' No man or woman can walk away from such a challenge without responding, even if only to play-argue. Now you have your audience…

Who else might be watching you?

- ❖ Remember always that although you may not be specifically interested in the person you are currently interacting with, someone you could be interested in may be observing you from close by. You always want to be presenting yourself as playful, confident, interesting, in control - and gracious.

Learn how to create an element of fascination.

- ❖ If you give your number/card to someone and don't want to appear that you do this all the time, say something like, 'here's my card because you're cute/handsome/charming (insert the word most appropriate for your situation), but don't ring me up in the middle of the night crying because you miss me…' and then wink. This singles you out as playful, implies your high value because they **would** miss you, and gives them a compliment too to encourage them - pleasure again.

So you've got past the first, second - and even third date and suddenly, you are starting to think about describing this as a relationship. Home and dry… Not so fast! Where could it go wrong?

Over-analysis:

He said, then I said, then he said back and I wondered… sound familiar? Women are particularly fond of trying to analyse and deduce - usually with the wrong conclusion, or at least one slanted by their previous experiences or influenced by their past prejudices. Over-analysis is trying to control what you can't control. Can you figure out all the permutations of what someone might be thinking or why they might be responding in a particular way? Let's try it: the guy asks you on a date and it goes well. You are expecting him to call and he doesn't. You wonder why, and come up with:

Over-analysis reasons	Possible other reasons
He didn't like me after all.	He's got a heavy week at work.
He's asking someone else out and comparing us.	He's ill.
I didn't look that good and I had a spot starting.	He's lost his phone or run out of credit.

He's a player.	He wasn't sure if you liked him.
He's married.	His Mum/Dad/kid/dog are ill.
He can't be bothered.	He's a slow mover - or maybe he's waiting to see what you'll do next?
I saw him online on that dating site we met through…	…And he saw you.

It's much easier to follow the principles of the Strategy and invest in him - or her - (because it applies equally to the guys as the girls, even though you guys don't tend to churn up all the possibilities like they're in a food mixer quite like the girls do) only what they invest in you. When they do get back to you, roll on the pleasure/pain principle as the big gun.

Neediness:

…Is all to do with insecurity and lack of core confidence: You are great as you are so project yourself and be proud of who you are. Neediness in itself is a very unattractive characteristic and if perceived in you, will put almost anyone off. When I was picking Pete's brains about things that were off-putting to guys, he told me a nice little cameo story which illustrated neediness perfectly.

'Ah neediness - that's a real turn-off!' He exclaimed, as soon as I mentioned the word. 'Did I ever tell you about this girl I met about a year ago who was exactly like that?'

I shook my head, but waited patiently for him to start - I could tell from the enlivened expression that Pete was about to go full flow now.

'She was actually quite nice and I was going to meet her again but she was really insistent that she wouldn't wait until the next week.'

'Why?' I was genuinely curious to see what Pete's analysis of this might be - over or under as it might be.

'I don't know - unless she thought she needed to nail me quick before anyone else did.' He preened himself whilst I silently called him an idiot, but acknowledged that actually if she was that needy, maybe that was exactly what she thought because she had no confidence in herself to maintain the attraction for him at a distance. True attraction would beat even a trip to the moon. I stayed silent so not to stop the rest of the story flow - not that there was much danger of that...

'Anyway, she agreed to something the following week as I was so busy and then she did it again at the end of the second date - and then again after the third one too. Eventually she asked me if we couldn't meet at least three times a week, how could we have a relationship? Then she asked me if I wanted a relationship with her. I guess she thought I would say yes.'

'And you said?'

'I said "not like this".' He looked smugly at me, as if waiting for my approval. I wasn't sure what to say back other than - 'what is a relationship for you then?'

'Well I don't want someone to try to take possession of me. You can have a relationship that blends two lives together, but not which completely controls one or both of them.'

For once, Pete the player had hit the nail on the head - and wanting to take over someone's life was surely because you didn't have the confidence in yourself to trust you were attractive enough as a person for them to want to blend their life with yours; back to insecurity again - and how being confident is sexy.

Being over-competitive:

Emasculates the person you're trying to impress, not attracts.

Jealousy:

Is the worst word in the whole dating dictionary: Jealousy comes from feeling like you're not as good as someone else. It means you're focussing on what you can't control. Say your date comments on how 'hot' someone is. As well as using your ability to frame behaviour by stating that there is nothing less hot than talking about someone else being hot in front of your date, remember that YOU are a unique package and your date has to *deserve* you. You may not be as beautiful or gifted as you perceive someone else to be, but you have your own package of gifts and talents, so never be jealous of what someone else has: be proud of what YOU have.

Jealousy is a destructive force and can develop in all kinds of situations, including those in which the participants didn't think there were any feelings to be involved at all to start with. Pete's most shocking story was his ultimate male fantasy story - told to me early on in our evenings out together. He boasted how he'd joined a dating site called something along the lines of 'be naughty'. Through it he met several ladies just for a romp, and his stories might really be more appropriate to the next chapter, but they also focussed ultimately on jealousy. You may think if you're just looking for a roll in the hay jealousy isn't going to be involved. It's just sex, isn't it? Wrong. Three people and a set of emotions don't work, whichever way you look at them. We were designed to partner up in pairs, not threes or fours or any other number under the sun, so of course jealousy ultimately reared its ugly head.

Pete met Elena first. It was described as a 'no strings' meeting, and initially the relationship went well - meet for sex, go home. Then along came Katrina. Katrina was younger, more attractive and sexier than Elena - and also looking for 'no strings'. Pete started to see both of them but eventually the pressure grew and he told both of them about the other. They met and got along and it slipped almost naturally into something akin to an electricity circuit, with Pete as the alternating current and the two girls as the AC and DC components as it soon became clear that Elena was confused about her sexuality and found Katrina as attractive as Pete did. Three-way sex ensued, and whilst it was shared equally: a bit of three-love, as opposed to free-love, all was well. They would meet and spend a cultural afternoon in the National Gallery and a markedly different one in the bedroom. But eventually the preferences one for another became apparent and then jealousy joined the network as an alternating current too. Now the three-way circuit started to break. Pete fancied Katrina, Elena fancied Katrina and Katrina fancied both Pete and Elena because she *wasn't* confused about her sexuality, and was prepared to switch responses whenever the resistance appeared less in one electrical flow than the other. Now I could consider the morality of threesomes until the National Grid ran dry, but what I really remarked upon was the power of jealousy. From Pete's descriptions of the spiteful and aggressive communications between the three of them, plainly its effect stretches beyond an emotional response into the whole fabric of how you behave, and it twists and warps otherwise straightforward physical responses. What Pete described as just sex became just vicious. I would describe it as all just destructive, and resulted in none of them speaking to each other eventually.

Of course jealousy isn't usually linked to such a complicated situation. It is usually simply one persons' irrationally insecure response to the fear of losing the power they thought they had when another person or influence joins in the party too. But whatever the reason the effect is distinctly unattractive.

I had to admit, Pete's tale also made him seem increasingly unattractive to me too. Where did this sit with my values? Did I have one that specified the number of partners anyone had at one time? Oh wait - I did - it was one.

Chapter 11: Let's talk about sex…

Let's start with assumption number one that men and women approach relationships from two different stances, pragmatic (men) and romantic (women). When a man thinks about a relationship, it includes a melee of immediate physical satisfaction in a comfortable situation. He doesn't want a 'difficult' or demanding woman, he wants a pleasant time. Truth or fiction? Let me go back to Pete's,

'… every date starts off as being a one night stand, but if it's good enough to be a one night stand, then maybe it should stretch to 2 or more…'

Well that comfortably seems to encapsulate the physical gratification idea. 'Sometimes, though,' he added, 'it can all be TOO quick,' even for the inclination for gratification first, question after, that men often have. To illustrate he recalled one of the dates he met in a central London Italian restaurant. After the meal and a pleasant evening of flirtation, she got up - he thought - to go to the ladies, but instead she proceeded to round the table and 'snog' him in the middle of the restaurant.

'Your place or mine?' immediately sprung to mind and she said 'yours' barely before he could ask it. They took a taxi back to his place and he politely went off to the kitchen to make the coffee. When he returned it was to a completely naked woman declining any sugar - she took it as it came... No comment of course from him - other than that he did see her a few times more and naturally they slept together again - no coffee involved, but there it ended. If men are assumed to be the sole instigators of the *sex now, talk later* attitude, where did this lady fit into it? Was she the exception that proves the rule or just part of the equation? Hmm, let's question this idea of the romantic woman: pragmatic man a little more.

I think I'm a romantic at heart, so what do I think about it all? I think that sex has a place within a relationship and that is not necessarily on the first or second or last date, but wherever it seems to fit with the way you feel *your partner is behaving towards you and the way you want to behave towards them*. So it is a joint effort. Mere gratification doesn't work - most women will complain they feel used afterwards, and most men will think it was too easy and devalue you, even if subconsciously, as a result. An interesting comment from another male friend a little while ago is very relevant here.

'We like to do a bit of chasing. We don't want to feel it was too easy to get there...'

So maybe that says, conversely, that sex on the first date might be what a man would look for in terms of physical gratification, but is it going to encourage him to look for more beyond that? Pete says maybe he'd go back for seconds, but seconds of what? He also told me of the many dates that involved sex at the end of the evening and he never saw or heard from them again. So what was the date for them? A disaster? A means to an end? Or another nail in the coffin of presumption and prejudice with them writing him off saying '... men are just all the same...'

I watched an acquaintance of mine almost being swallowed whole by a woman not that long ago. He knew she was dating another guy - even stood next to her in the pub as she and the guy virtually stripped each other and had sex on the table, their hands and tongues were in so many places at once. I and others looked on at the show with curiosity. So did he, yet he also persistently attempted to flirt with her, and she, of course, flirted back. Then she told him which singles event she would be at next and he dutifully turned up, and pursued her all evening until she relented and they sat at a table on their own, hands clasped, looking into each other's eyes and intermittently kissed; full-on passion. I again watched from my vantage point amongst friends, knowing that she would, self-admittedly, be dating the other guy tomorrow night, and doing the same with him. I didn't know whether the other guy knew what she was doing - probably not as he'd seemed blissfully unaware when I'd last seen them together: the kind of blissful unawareness that didn't even register that there was another guy flirting with his date whenever he went to the bar or the loo. He just smiled at him as if he were a mate standing nearby. But my acquaintance knew, and still he was utterly smitten - or maybe he just knew when he was onto a good non-commitment thing?

Now that raises two interesting ideas; first, how do we - men **and** women, that is - fall in love, and what role does sex play in it.

Love is something we all want, but often feel like we have to work very hard to get. That makes it valuable. It follows then that you have to be valuable to your partner for them to want to 'get' you. And when I say 'get' you, I mean get hold of you for keeps, and also really 'get' the inner you - the one that is valuable, and that they need to get to know in order to love you.

We all remember our pride in our first car - the one we had to save like mad to be able to afford, or the job we so wanted when the interview was an absolute *bitch*, or the qualification that we had to study night and day for. We had to work hard to earn any of those things. If someone had just come along and said, 'here you go, have this…' Would any of those things been as dear to us, or as important? So if a guy or a girl says 'yes, ok' to sex on the first date - do we value or devalue them?

Ladies: Here's an important thing to know about men –

'A guy wants to feel like he's significant to a woman and that she likes him so much that he is special enough to share something as intimate as sex with him.'

Quote me on that, if you like. It's straight from a guy. Every good guy answering the question: 'what do you think about a woman who has sex with you? What makes her worth having a relationship with?' would agree.

So when is the right time to have sex?
As usual where emotions are concerned there is no definitive length of string, no matter how long it is (the string, you smutty people!) It seems to work roughly like this though:
- ✓ **There has to be a 'connection' between the two of you.** Not necessarily time, but intensity and shared experience creates a connection; an emotional shift that turns them from someone you like to someone you LIKE.
- ✓ **There's an emotional shift** that takes you from dating to sleeping with… Maybe you spend a lot of time over a short period and think that has enabled intensity between you - but what are they like when they're grumpy? What do they think of you when you're down? Does the intensity of feeling survive the ups and downs of daily life? That's the connection.
- ✓ **When you feel you can trust and rely on someone**, then you can trust them sufficiently to also share your body with them.

Foreplay – does it count?

'If she's a rubbish kisser, I just won't go there…'

  Pete, as usual had a strong opinion on foreplay, but I've heard other men and women say exactly the same thing. Let's look at the opinions. Foreplay is the lead in to sex and tells you many things about the person you are potentially going to sleep with. If you don't enjoy their kisses - are you going to enjoy them kissing you whilst making love? Can you simply say 'no kissing'? Of course not. It does give you an idea of whether you are physically compatible - and attraction is made up of both physical and emotional responses. If you don't fancy them, it's very hard to get beyond first base, no matter how many strikes you have at it.

Foreplay is also exactly what it says on the tin - the play before full sex, so for how long do you play the game and how much of it should you play before sex is the next step? For each of us foreplay includes different levels. For some it's simply kissing. For others it's kissing and fondling. Maybe for you it's kissing, fondling and some intimate touching too. For others, could it go as far even as oral sex? Ultimately this is a personal decision and you have to decide on your own level - the level you're prepared to go to and which sits comfortably within your value structure. If it's not the same as his - or guys, hers isn't the same as yours - then you need to be prepared to openly and honestly compare and maybe come to a compromise. And if you're already learning how to agree compromises with each other, taking into account each other's value systems, then you're well on the way to that connection, anyway, aren't you?

Do guys lose interest after sex?

Pete? You're a typical red-blooded alpha male - what do you say?
    Actually he said it quite early on, I remembered.

'... if it's good enough to be a one night stand then maybe it should stretch to 2 or more...'

Ok, so Pete started out from the basis of it being a one-night stand, but what I decided he really meant was that, if the person you were sleeping with was 'special' for you, then you didn't lose interest after just one night together. Special - aka connected...

If, on the other hand, the guy does lose interest straight away, what might be the reasons?

- One night stands are just that - for one night. From the guys point of view, if you do this with him as soon as you meet him, how many other guys have you done it with, and consecutively? Does that make you girlfriend material? (Answers on a micro-chip, please).
- First date sex is often no good anyway - you don't know them and what they like, they don't know you and what you like - much better over time...
- Embarrassment: It may well have been the product of a drunken mistake - the easiest thing of all afterwards when you're embarrassed at what you've done, is to 'bugger off' as one guy nicely put it!
- Sex was used by the girl as a lure, but now the guy has enjoyed the prize, the lure is gone. Never use sex as a tool to try to lure a guy - you create an interest in the act of sex, but not in you.

Another guy quote: 'Sex is meaningless if the situation is meaningless...'

Sex before commitment: is that ok?

Only if the following apply:

- ✓ It is within your value system to do so.
- ✓ You are also doing other things together too, which aren't solely revolving around sex - in other words it is just part of the way you are getting to know each other on the way to a committed relationship.
- ✓ Only if you're the only one they're doing it with, otherwise why are you being part of a team?
    - ✗ **Not** if they only do things with you that lead to sex, or they intend to lead to sex. There's no inclination then to turn it into a relationship eventually if they're already getting all they require without one.

Girls: how do you know if a guy is just using you for sex?

- ✗ He won't follow up but will delay, postpone, cut dates UNLESS they are likely to lead to sex.
- ✗ He's not interested in 'sandwich' dates where no sex would be possible - for example coffee on a Saturday morning in town will get passed on (where would you go for sex?) whereas Friday night drinks at the pub across the road from his place (we all know where you'd go fu'ckoffee, don't we?) would be a dead cert.

☒ From how he reacts to you saying no…

Is sex all men think about?

Unfortunately the answer to that is largely – yes… but, let's look at the reasons why. Let's go back to those man-speak/women-speak definitions from Chapter 5: The cynical amongst us could also add some of the following from the pragmatic guys we've met from time to time…

Do you want to go to a movie? - *I'd eventually like to have sex with you.*

Can I take you out to dinner? - *I'd eventually like to have sex with you.*

Would you like to dance? - *I'd eventually like to have sex with you.*

Can I call you sometime? - *I'd eventually like to have sex with you.*

Nice dress! - *I'd eventually like to have sex with you.*

You look tense, let me give you a massage - *I'd eventually like to have sex with you.*

You look upset - *I guess sex tonight is out of the question…*

(But as an aside, if you were out on a date with a man you fancied, would you really want him to be thinking, 'I hope I don't have to have sex with her…'?)

Anyway, why do men think about it so much? Well it is all to do with biological make-up and self-worth. Men are the hunter-gatherers, the protectors, the strong, and able - they peacock to the less dominant of the species; the females, and their sense of self-worth is heavily invested in their sexual prowess. It IS the archetypal expression of their maleness. They are also basically physical creatures whereas women are emotional - pragmatic v romantic. Sex therefore appeals to their:

Mmmmm – sense of pleasure.

Grrr- rarrr - sense of male impetus - the big strong man.

Ok, I do that too - social and media influences, newspapers, ads, magazines, 007 and so on.

*Ok I **can** do that too* - their sense of self-worth. Men base their self-worth on how sexually desirable they are.

How many women do you hear boasting about how many men they've slept with this week? None (I hope). Sleeping around isn't seen as an attractive feminine trait, but with a guy, men regard sexual prowess as proving their manliness. If he wants to sleep with you ladies, accept it as a compliment - and a bit of peacocking. As long as you say no until you want to say yes, all is well. BUT it's not all men think about - so apart from multi-tasking to think about sex + food or sex + football, when it comes down to the woman they want in their life, they are also working out whether you demonstrate all the other criteria they have which convert you from potential sex partner to actual girlfriend material too.

Is sex meaningful for men?

Yes of course it is, just as it is meaningful for a woman - if you're connected (and not in the obvious way). It has emotional impact on a man as much as it does on a woman as an expression of loving and caring and sharing. Shared intense experiences are what create a connection and then make both people in the relationship want to go further.

What you do straight after sex makes a big difference. It either makes it a special shared experience, with time to follow up on the closeness, or a mere alternative to having gone to the gym. If one or both of you just go home afterwards, then there is no sharing. It takes two to make it a special experience and a stating of values from both sides to make sure it doesn't become merely 'just sex'.

What does a guy think about after sex?

'I need to sleep.' It's hard exercise, and men are physical beings, remember?
'Was I ok?'
'Was this any good?'
'Did she enjoy it?'
Because how he performs sexually is such an important part of a guy's sense of self-worth, his biggest fear is failure. When we care about someone we reassure them when they need it and build them up. For a woman, it is important to remember that her partner needs as much encouragement as she does.

How do you show a guy what you like?

Don't be shy. He'd much rather you weren't otherwise he's as much in the dark as if you've turned the lights off. Incidentally, don't (turn the lights off, that is). It makes him think you're embarrassed about your body, or about his and that's very inhibiting. Appreciative noises or comments are fine - come on girls, practice - 'mmm', 'oooh'...

If that doesn't work, there's nothing like leading a horse to water. Either show him, or guide him, or tell him. Honest explanation should be becoming a regular feature of your relationship already if you're comfortable sleeping together. If you can explain the importance of your principles and values to him, then a few little sex tips are nothing.

Comment afterwards - 'that thing you did... was great...'

Say 'I like it so much when you...,' not 'if you did..., that would be great,' because that suggests he didn't do very well and his sense of self-worth will be compromised.

And anyway - what about framing required sexual behaviour? Model what you want in the same way you model other behaviour. Respond to what you like enthusiastically, don't to what you don't. He'll soon get the picture.

The biggest sexual mistakes a woman can make?

Irritating his male insecurity:

Having sex too soon - rushing over the barriers as if it was a race.

Devaluing yourself to him, self-deprecating comments about your looks or by having sex too quickly with him.

Using sex as a power tool - leave that for Ann Summers.

Not being a 'prize' he wants to win.

Punishing him for perceived wrongs by withholding sex.

Delaying too long before having sex - sometimes waiting can go on for too long and a guy will believe it's never going to go anywhere between you as a result. If someone else comes along in the meantime, giving all the right signals, then...

Continuing, if he's not investing and committing. There is no such thing as a 'friends with benefits' *relationship.* You are just being used.

In a relationship: lack of frequency. Men need sex. If it's withheld, or tails off because a woman loses interest, then the relationship will start to rapidly deflate with the guys' ego. Sex IS part of a normal healthy relationship. If for some reason one or both of you aren't enjoying or wanting it, it is time to examine the underlying reasons and get some help sorting them out.

In a relationship: getting stale. Earlier I commented on how the same old thing becomes the boring old thing. That's what can take you automatically into the friend's zone - you are not stimulating and interesting. The same can happen with sex. Routine sex is like doing the chores. Keep it new and exciting. Maybe the fantasies your guy says he wants to play out don't appeal, but remember a large part of it is the fact that it is a fantasy that makes it attractive to him - remember how he wants to win the prize? It makes it high value. Never say never, say *maybe* - it'll keep him guessing, and he'll probably never do more than mention it ever again.

Lack of body confidence is a killer - for him and for you. If you think you have a fat stomach and keep mentioning it he will become wary of drawing attention to it and then it becomes a no-go area. Do you want no-go areas on your body? Remember, this guy fancies you enough to want to sleep with you. Nothing on you is unattractive or no-go, so go for it all!

The biggest sexual mistakes a man can make?

Foreplay is an essential part of enjoyable sex for a woman. Take careful note of its description 'fore' so it happens first - and for as long as it takes. Forget that at your peril...

No personal comments please, unless they're compliments. Do you want a woman who's neurotic about her body? Or one who's confident and adventurous?

There is a G spot for every woman, but it may be in a different place to your last partners'. Take the time to find the right place, and be guided or ask. Don't assume because you're so dextrous on your play station controls that you're hitting the target with your partner too.

Men are very competitive beings, but in this one instance, it definitely pays to come second.

After the event: Women like to cuddle (and annoyingly, talk - sometimes really stupid gooey stuff); put up with it. It pays dividends in the long term. One of the hormonal differences in women to men is that whilst both male and female bodies are suffused with a hormone called oxytocin straight after sex and this creates a bonding effect, where men simply feel the need for sleep, women want to carry on being intimate. It is an important part of the 'connection' for a woman, so don't overlook it as the zeds try to take over.

Finally, women's bodies are infinitely more complex than men's, and remember they have the additional complication of hormonal changes every month. Sometimes there may be a genuine reason for her lack of passion, so talk about it. Don't just get the hump. The more you communicate, the better your relationship will be, including the sexual one.

Remember: When the sex life, dies, the relationship follows soon after.

And a few little hints and tips on preferences to end with.

Girls, about the guys:

1. Oral is king: Basically speaking, oral sex falls under the headings of "just wanting to get off" and "it's kinkier" than regular sex. Men know that it usually takes more work to get a woman to orgasm than a man, so if it's just about him, oral sex means that gratification is merely moments away

2. Acupressure arousal: According to the Chinese therapy of acupressure, there are a number of communication channels running throughout the human body. A man's most carnal channel is from his big toe, to the top of his foot and along the inside of his leg, so applying pressure with your palm along these areas will stimulate him more than other areas.

3. It Doesn't Pay to Be Passive or quiet: Some women still feel that the man should take charge, or are too shy to speak up during sex. But girls, this is your body, and you know it better than anyone else, so enjoy it - and there's nothing sexier to a man than a woman who knows about pleasure.

Guys - here's a couple of important things to know about the girls:

4. Apparently a woman's breasts swell up to 25% during good sex. This is her body's way of seducing/attracting/urging the man to finish with a finale, so don't disappoint her (but don't get the tape measure out either or she might use it on you too).

5. There are two G spots: One internally and one externally - stereo. If you take the time to find both, its fireworks every time!

WHAT MAKES the spark in the dark?

Body confidence

Sexual confidence

Honesty - about your preferences

Patience

Communication

Open-mindedness

Playfulness

Variety

Frequency

Reciprocity

I suppose Pete's comments about sleeping with someone on a first date infuriated me, and yet, sex is a BIG part of relationships. It's is a tricky old subject too. We all do it, and it has a very essential part in any relationship between a man and women - even the ones you're not dating. There are never really 'just good friends' between men and women, there is always an underlying current that reminds us that we are two different sexes and we were designed to react with each other just as spontaneously as nuclear fission, and often with similar fall-out.

Sex and falling in love - the drug fix:

When a man and woman have an orgasm, it releases a flood of the chemical oxytocin directly into their bloodstream. It's a clever little chemical - as clever as those mirror neurons, but it has some similarity too, in that it creates mirror image responses in men and women. However this time the mirror images are precisely that - the opposite.

'Oxytocin seems to have been 'designed' by nature to make a man and woman feel bonded after sex, but oestrogen (in women) seems to increase the bonding effects of oxytocin, while testosterone (in men) seems to mute them. That's why women tend to feel more attached after sex than men do.'(6)

Unfortunately men not only often feel less attached than women, but completely unattached or disinterested in the woman they've just slept with. All of a sudden we have the scientific reason why he is suddenly too busy to see or even call, and may even begin to avoid her. In true mirror-image form, the woman is also flooded with all sorts of other chemicals in addition to oxytocin. PEA or Phenylethylamine, and chemicals such as dopamine and serotonin surge after she has sex with a man, often resulting in her feeling deeply attached and desperate for more of him. Oh dear.

If men and women's reactions are so different after sex, how and when can sex and love co-exist? The answer lies in yet another chemical: endorphins. Over time, as the emotional bond of sharing and caring builds between a man and woman, endorphins are released in both of them, and these chemicals are responsible for long-term bonding. So that exhortation to wait has as much basis in science as initial attraction has. All you girls who go for sex as soon as you meet; be careful what you wish for, and all you guys who accept gladly - you deserve all the hassle you get!

Chapter 12: The bitter end - or the beautiful beginning

Success in life is all about being true to yourself; finding the confidence within yourself to take opportunities in both hands when they appear, and to enjoy it all. Life doesn't have to be driven by finding or having a romantic partner, although it is our natural inclination to be a pair, instead of a singleton. However if it's your goal in life to find your mate, then make sure the way you set about it is fun. Then even if you don't ultimately find the one that lasts a lifetime, the ones you do find make life good whilst you're together, and the way you set about it makes it enjoyable in the meantime. You are an amazing person and you deserve someone equally amazing for you. Never forget that.

Confidence comes in layers:

The surface layer is what everyone sees – but vulnerable, as it may be only on the surface.

The Lifestyle layer is everything you do in our life that gives you confidence and security – but vulnerable, because at any point you may lose it - your job, your home, your relationship.

The core level is the thing that remains and gives you confidence whatever happens. It is who you understand yourself to be.

When you're out dating, you need to employ all the layers to achieve your goal, but at the end of it all it is what lies beneath, and where my experiences with Pete first started me - your values, standards and principles. They're what make you that VSP - Very Sexy Person, who is going out there with a strategy - a plan: how to win at the dating game.

Success is growth on level you want it. Sometimes when you look carefully at yourself, you can find the growth you wanted once is different as an adult to that as a child. Sometimes trying to find a good date or the right partner feels like a battle, but if you're doing the right things, the battle is won whilst you're still single.

I tried the rest of the whole strategy out on Pete, when he next asked me out on another date, but despite the fact that he was all ears, eyes and attention now, I found I no longer was. Having established my VSP, it was a different woman to who I'd thought I was. Sadly for Pete, I politely left him at the bar, paying the bill, as I found my car in the car park. A text came in from Alex - the bodyguard, asking if I might need minding again at the weekend.

'Well, ironically, you've just picked a time when I'm unexpectedly free...'

Want to try it out for yourself?

Time to play here then...

The work it out for yourself bit:

Fill in, leave out or just doodle, as you wish…

Section 1 - the whys, whats, wheres and hows…

First of all: the whys? Well I suppose there were a number of 'whys':

- Why did I want a guy?
- Why did I want THIS particular guy?
- Why wasn't he interested in me? He liked me in a roundabout way but, here I was in friend zone…
- Why did I get relegated to friend's zone in the first place?
- Why if he didn't like me in the right way, did I never meet anyone who did?

My 'why's' are:

....
....
....
....
....
....
....
....
....
....
....
....
....

Then there were some 'whats':

- What was the matter with me?...Ouch, that one felt quite uncomfortable!
- What was I doing wrong?
- What should I be doing instead?
- What exactly was I aiming to achieve?

My 'what's' are:

....
....
....
....
....
....
....
....
....
....
....
....
....
....
....

Then there were the 'how's':

- How do I change my behaviour pattern, if that is the problem?
- How do I change men's perception of me?

- How do I find the kind of man I would like to meet?
- How do I convince him he's interested in ME?
- (of course this included Pete at the time) How did I get Pete to be interested in me?)
- How did I keep them interested?

My 'how's' are:

....
....
....
....
....
....
....
....
....
....
....
....
....
....
....
....
....
....
....

And finally there were the' wheres':

- Where do I go to do any of this...?
- Where will I find the information to complete my strategy?

My 'where's' are:

Section 2 Values - careful what you wish for...

What are yours?

A handy bit of page to try scribbling them down, then value, devalue, value, devalue as often as you like until you think you've got them all.

Principle	Value	Standard	How it may be demonstrated

Now some trickier stuff:

If there are standards there you don't like and which don't reflect your internal values? What are they?

....
....
....
....
....
....
....
....
....

Are they learned patterns of behaviour from role models or past experience you think you could shift so they more closely reflect your real, internally held, values?
If so, how will you make the shifts to remove or change them: How would you do that for each of them?

....
....
....
....
....
....
....
....
....
....

Now you've shifted the bad bits - what are the fantastic bits about you that you really want to promote more?

....
....
....
....
....
....
....
....
....
....
....

How are you going to do that? Some hints: make it practical suggestions you can definitely cope with. Smaller steps are better than big ones that are too off-putting when you come to tackle them. Remember those SMART targets are best.

....
....
....
....
....
....
....
....
....
....

Now determine what the most important values are in the type of guy or girl you'd like to meet, and how you expect them demonstrated in their values.

Principle	Value	Standard	How it may be demonstrated

Section 3: the Man-nav or Sat-girl - what are the stopping points on your route?

Here's the A to Z.

Select the values and attributes you'd like and check out the kind of places you may find that type of person.

Alphabet	Places	Likely values/attributes
A	*Art gallery*	cultural
B	Book club	Cultural
	Bars	Lively, social, party animal
	Business networking	Career orientated, professional
	Beach	Social, sporty
	Bowling	Sporty but light hearted
	Bingo	Less active
	Barbecues	Social and outdoorsy
C	Cycling club	Sporty, specific interest
	Coffee shop	Social
	Comic book club	Specific interests
	Comedy club	Light hearted and social
	Ceroc	Loves dancing
	Clubs (see bars)	Lively, social, party animal
	Conventions for hobbies/interests	Specific interests
	Conferences	Career orientated, professional, Specific interests
	Cocktail bars	Social, lively, party animal
	Classes	Personal growth orientated, and specific interest
	Car boot sales	Practical, material, sociable

D	*Dog walking*	Loves dogs, walking, outdoorsy, sociable
	Dance classes – all sorts	Loves dancing, sociable, active
	Debating clubs	Cultural, intellectual, articulate, social, confident
E	Exercise classes	Specific interest, sporty, looks after self
	Edinburgh Fringe	Sense of humour, unusual, cultural
	Elevator (lift)	Sociable
	Exhibitions	Cultural, intellectual
	Electronics store – eg Apple	Geeky, but very male
	Evening classes	Self growth, specific interest
F	Folk club	Specific musical interest
	Fairs (misc types eg mystic, steam etc)	Specific interests
	Festivals	Specific interests, and often music lovers – various
	Football matches	The obvious one for 1000s of men!
	Flower markets	Social, specific interests
	(through) Friends	Social – and anything is possible!
G	*Gym*	Sporty, looks after self
	Golf	Specific interest
	Gardens	Specific interest
	Garden centres	Specific interest
H	Health club	Sporty, looks after self
	Horse riding	Specific interest
	Health food shop	Specific interest
	Hotel foyers and bars- or any foyers	Sociable
I	*Internet*	Anything is possible but read 'Are you the one?' first!
	Ikea	Sociable
	Ice skating	Specific interest, sporty, sociable, fun

J	Jive dancing	Loves dancing and sociable
	Jazz clubs	Sociable and specific interest
K	Kick Boxing	Male orientated, sporty
	Kayaking	Sporty, specific interest
	Karaoke bars	Sociable, extrovert, maybe an exhibitionist
L	Line dancing	Specific interest
	Library	Self-growth, love reading, intellectual, cultural
	Lido	Swimming, social
	Lectures	Self-growth, specific interest, intellectual, cultural
M	*Museums*	Self-growth, specific interest, intellectual, cultural
	Meet-up groups	Social – anything could be involved
	markets	social
N	*Night clubs*	Social, lively, party animal
	Night school	Self-growth, specific interest, intellectual, cultural
	Neighbours	Who knows – anything could happen!
O	Opera	Intellectual, cultural, music lover
P	*Pubs*	Social, lively,
	Parties	Social lively, party animal
	Public speaking groups	Self-growth, specific interest, Intellectual, cultural
	Parks	Outdoorsy, social
	Public lectures	Self-growth, specific interest, intellectual, cultural
	Photography club	Specific interest
Q	Quiz night	Quiz night, likes challenges, social
	Queues	Social – anything could happen
R	*Restaurants*	Social, lively food lover
	Races	Likes a flutter and an occasion,

		specific interest, social
	Record shops	Social and music lover
	Rowing clubs	Specific interest and sporty
	Rugby	Specific interest and sporty
S	Salsa	Loves dancing, social
	Supermarkets	Social – anything could happen
	Shopping	Social – anything could happen
	Sailing	Specific interest
	Speed dating	Social, lively and anything could happen
	Secret cinema club	Specific interest
	Specialist conventions (eg are you a trekkie?)	Specific interest
T	Tennis club	Specific interest and sporty
	Toastmaster groups	Self-growth, intellectual, social
U	*University*	Self-growth, intellectual, social
	Underbelly festival	Self-growth, intellectual, social
	Urban golf	Specific interest, sporty, social
V	Volunteering	Self-growth, intellectual, social, a giver
	Volley ball (on the beach)	Social, sporty
W	Walking clubs	Enjoys walking, sporty, social
	Writers groups	Intellectual, specific interest, cultural
	Wine tasting groups	Specific interest, social
	Whisky tasting class	Specific interest, social, Scottish
	Wine bars	Social, lively, party animal
	Waterstones	Enjoys reading, intellectual, cultural specific interests

	Watersports	Specific interest, sporty
X	Xtreme sports clubs	Specific interest, mad
Y	Yoga – Bikram or Ashtanger best	Self-growth, looks after self
	Yachting	Specific interest, sporty
	Laughter yoga	Self-growth, looks after self, social
Z	Zoo lates – at Zoos in London from 2012	Loves animals, specific interest

Now you've decided what appeals, the next stop is to look online or through your local magazines, newspapers, at your tourist information offices or local council offices for any information about groups which may be relevant. Also don't forget Meet-ups - there are meet-up groups springing up all over the place for all kinds of things. Browse the possibilities. You could even start your own, or join a singles group like the one I run (www.singlesthatmingle.co.uk) for all kinds of events and opportunities. Here's a space for a list for the first ones you're going to try:

....
....
....
....
....
....
....
....

Section 4: Hello I'm….

So you like it /don't like it - but what about yourself do you include that is holding you back or could push you forward? Here's a chance to pin it down - and remember to repeat it from time to time. No matter how well we start out, we often slip into another routine, and need to get rid of that one too a bit further down the line…

I like about me…	I dislike about me…	What can I do with this?	How can I change this?

Talking yourself up not down:

Ask yourself these questions:

- **Why do I think I'm not good enough/ can't do it?**

....
....
....
....

- **Who has told me that in the past?**

....
....
....

- **Were they jealous or in competition with you - or even just wanted to have the upper hand** *in some way?*

....
....
....
....

- **Were they right or did you prove them wrong?**

....
....
....
....

- **Who else do I know who regularly overcomes obstacles and difficulties?**

....
....
....
....

- **How do they do it?**

....
....
....
....

- **When where the times I was right/was good enough?**

....
....
....

Now write some 'talk yourself up' phrases to remember- whatever reminds you of your biggest success:

....
....
....

Getting social - my action plan is to:

Where to go and what to do: start with what is easy for you, and doesn't entail walking in, and announcing yourself to the world: Month 1 - is one per week, then next month, it's two per week, then by month three, you're an old hand it - and go for three or more.

- Join a class...

    1..

    2..

    3..

- Join a club...

    1..

    2..

    3..

- Volunteer to help out at something you think important…

    1……………………………………………………………………

    2……………………………………………………………………

    3……………………………………………………………………

- Enlist a friend to go somewhere new…

    1……………………………………………………………………

    2……………………………………………………………………

    3……………………………………………………………………

- Smile at whoever you meet
- Say yes to all invitations to events or social meetings
- Start a ritual (remember those from chapter 3?) to talk to one new person a day wherever you are. My rituals are…

    1……………………………………………………………………

    2……………………………………………………………………

    3……………………………………………………………………

- Make yourself a social hub - hold a 'happy-hour' get together regularly, invite everyone along to it - at a local bar or pub, or convenient meeting point. Ask friends and colleagues to bring friends and colleagues and a watch your network grow.

Make a list of the friends you'd like to invite:

……………………………………………………………………………………………………

……………………………………………………………………………………………………

……………………………………………………………………………………………………

……………………………………………………………………………………………………

……………………………………………………………………………………………………

……………………………………………………………………………………………………

……………………………………………………………………………………………………

Now make a list of places you could arrange for your regular 'happy hour'.

……………………………………………………………………………………………………

……………………………………………………………………………………………………

……………………………………………………………………………………………………

……………………………………………………………………………………………………

……………………………………………………………………………………………………

That seems like a social plan to me!

Bibliography and references:

1. Aristotle: Philosopher, scientist and physician 384BC – 322BC
2. Debbie Martin (me!)
3. Gallese, V., Fadiga, L., Fogassi, L. & Rizzolatti, G. (1996). Action recognition in the premotor cortex. *Brain*, 119, 593-609.
4. Rizzolatti, G. (2005). The mirror neuron system and its function in humans. *Anatomy and Embryology*, 210, 419-421.
5. Matthew Hussey in his Get the Guy 'Women's Weekend' April 2012
6. Susan Kuchinskas: author of *The Chemistry of Connection: How the Oxytocin response can help you find trust, intimacy and love*, (2009)